THE OTHER
Notting Hill

THE OTHER
Notting Hill

CHRIS HOLMES

BREWIN BOOKS

First published by
Brewin Books Ltd, 56 Alcester Road,
Studley, Warwickshire B80 7LG in 2005
www.brewinbooks.com

ISBN 1 85858 264 4

The moral right of the author has been asserted.

A Cataloguing in Publication Record
for this title is available from the British Library.

Typeset in Plantin
Printed in Great Britain by
The Cromwell Press

CONTENTS

ACKNOWLEDGEMENTS

I would like to thank the Notting Hill Housing Group for commissioning me to write this history to mark its 40th anniversary, and for all the assistance they have given with the project.

I would like to thank everyone who agreed to be interviewed for the book: Geeta Ahluwalia, Arwa Al-Shabib, Sue Black, Mary Burke, David Campion, John Coward, Phyliss Danny, Peter Dixon, John Gregory, Alan Fell, Madeleine Jeffery, Sarah Harrison, Mary Harvey, Steve Hilditch, Sam Hood, Donald Hoodless, Nick Hughes, Penny Hutton, Bruce Kenrick, Isabel Kenrick, Annabel Louvros, Lionel Morrison, Kate Morton, Adrian Norridge, Peter Redman, Lea Richardson, Ingrid Reynolds, Dudley Savill, Jo Simpson, Roz Spencer, Roger Tuson, Michael White, Pat White, Jenny Williams and Andrew Williamson.

I am very grateful to all the members of the Steering Group for their advice at all stages of the project, including their helpful comments on successive drafts. John Coward, Martin Prater and Anthony Taussig also provided valuable notes on some key events and Martin Prater has generously shared with me the results of his own research into the archives and provided invaluable tables on the Trust's finances, housing stock and and fundraising.

I am also very grateful to Michael White for his revisions to the draft, especially in improving the style and the political and social comments.

Finally, I would like to thank my partner, Hattie Llewelyn-Davies for her support at every stage in researching and writing the book, including her many helpful comments and suggestions on the text.

Chris Holmes
September 2004

INTRODUCTION

This book was commissioned by the Notting Hill Housing Group to mark the 40th anniversary of the Trust. It does not aim to be a comprehensive chronological record of each of the past forty years. It focuses especially on events in the first fifteen years, which saw the birth of the Trust in an inner city area of severe housing stress and its development into one of the country's leading housing associations. It also describes how the Trust has adapted over the past forty years, in response to major social, economic and political changes, and to the changing legislative and financial frameworks in which housing associations work.

It is a study of the Trust, but also of the social history of the area where it has worked. In the early 1960s the Notting Hill area, in West London, had gained national notoriety for the activities of the private landlord, Peter Rachman, in exploiting vulnerable tenants. Thousands of private tenants were living in decaying, multi-occupied and overcrowded homes. As property speculators saw the potential for gentrification, existing tenants faced the threat of eviction and homelessness.

In response to this crisis, a huge community campaign was launched to change the housing policies of the local authority. After intensive arguments, and some dramatic confrontations between the different protagonists, the Council embraced an ambitious new strategy for tackling the housing problems. The Trust played a pivotal role, emerging as the agency charged with acquiring and renovating homes in a ground-breaking plan of community-based housing renewal.

Another important ingredient in the narrative was the consequence of the settlement in Notting Hill of black migrants from the Caribbean; the defensive, and on occasions, violent response of some members of the white community; and how the area came to attain symbolic importance for West Indians well beyond the boundaries of North Kensington.

The Trust was started by the Rev Bruce Kenrick in December 1963, and quickly made a huge impact with radio and television appeals and a powerful advertising campaign, which showed striking photographs of a family of six sharing a single room. This publicity was followed by the demanding task of building an organisation for buying and converting properties to provide homes for people in need.

Three years later Bruce Kenrick played the leading role in the creation of Shelter, fired by a vision of the need for a national homelessness campaign. Sadly, he resigned from his position as Chair of Shelter's trustees within a few months of its launch, as the result of internal tensions. As a result, the importance of his role was not publicly recognised. This book tells for the first time the real story of how Shelter came into existence.

The Notting Hill Housing Trust was a leading member of the new wave of charitable housing associations, mostly renovating run-down older properties in inner city areas and providing homes for families trapped in overcrowded, multi-occupied accommodation.

As a result of its work, the Trust had an important influence on the framing of the bipartisan 1974 Housing Act, including the new funding arrangements for housing associations and the powers for local authorities to declare Housing Action Areas in neighbourhoods of housing stress.

The years after 1974 were a period of rapid and sustained growth for the Trust. In North Kensington much of the development work was in the Colville and Tavistock area, the first Housing Action Area to be declared in the country. In the neighbouring borough of Hammersmith and Fulham, the Trust was asked by the Council to become the lead housing association in ten Housing Action Areas, one of the largest programmes in the country.

The Trust was the pioneer of community leasehold, and developed the first shared ownership scheme by a housing association which was opened in July 1979. The Trust set up a subsidiary, the Addison Housing Association, which developed a growing programme in the 1980s and 1990s, and became one of the housing association leaders in low cost home ownership.

Throughout the Trust's 40 years there have been two activities which have supplemented the reliance on statutory income and the work of paid staff. These are the large sums of money that have been raised through fundraising activity and the many hours given by volunteers. As well as the direct benefits, these have had an importance influence on the ethos of the Trust as a voluntary organisation.

The Trust moved into a different phase following the election of a new Conservative Government under Margaret Thatcher, a government whose first priority was the growth of home ownership and which was less committed to the development of socially rented housing.

The 1988 Housing Act heralded major changes in the way housing associations funded new developments. It became impossible for the Trust to buy street properties, and virtually all development activity was in building new homes or renovating run-down blocks of flats. Housing associations increasingly had to bid against each other for new projects, under pressure to reduce costs and develop only on cheaper sites. It meant that rents increased rapidly, with more tenants dependent on housing benefit.

The Trust had to learn new skills for managing housing estates with large numbers of non-earning and vulnerable tenants. In response it developed policies for new forms of estate design, the integration of different tenures, and community development initiatives to promote sustainable neighbourhoods.

The Notting Hill Housing Group - the name now used for the Trust and its subsidiary arms - now works in a very different environment from that of the Trust's early years. The housing conditions are very different. The kind of overcrowding and sharing that prevailed in run-down, privately rented homes of the Rachman era is now almost unknown. It has been replaced by severe overcrowding in local authority and housing association properties, as the scarcity of housing in an overheated London housing market makes it almost impossible to transfer tenants to larger homes.

Many more people own their homes, but whilst escalating house prices have benefited existing owners they have made it far harder for people on middle incomes to find anywhere affordable to live. They have also significantly widened the gap between rich and poor. Even where homeless families are housed by associations such as Notting Hill in homes leased from private landlords, these lack the stability of permanent homes, and children may face several moves to different schools.

The Group now owns or manages 18,000 homes, and is one of the largest housing associations in the country. The number of shared ownership and temporary homes is almost equal to the stock of long-term tenancies.

A key question is how much has been gained or lost in the past 40 years? In its first decade the Trust was a ground-breaking pioneer, a brave, fledgling organisation battling to provide decent homes for desperate people, with little experience, few allies, and inadequate resources.

What it achieved in those early years was remarkable, and a major task for this book is to record the history of how it was achieved. But is it now just that – history – with little relevance for the present and the future? Or are there lessons to be learnt from that history, which can inspire and help to guide those who plan what the Group does in the future?

This book is the history of one housing association, but it can also be a prism through which the history of the wider housing movement over the past forty years can be seen. Every housing association is unique, and Notting Hill has had an exceptionally interesting life. But many other associations have also lived through the huge changes in the external environment – financial, legislative, social and political.

There are a significant number of associations which were set up in the 1960s, with similar roots to the Notting Hill Housing Trust. There are many individuals who shared a similar vision and values to those which inspired the creators of the Trust. They too wanted to do what they could to make the world a better place, and believed that providing good quality affordable homes is one very important way of doing it.

Chapter 1

NOTTING HILL IN THE 1960s

The popularity of the film "Notting Hill" has given the area a world-wide image as a glamorous, exciting, desirable place to live. Notting Hill in the 1960s was very different. It was home to residents with a huge range of incomes and backgrounds, a minority were well off, but most were poor.

The southern end of the area comprised mostly large properties, including highly desirable residential squares, occupied by well-off owner-occupiers. To the north and west were several housing association and local authority estates, mostly accommodating well-established, white, working class residents. The majority of the dwellings in the rest of the area were owned by private landlords.

There were a large number of private tenants, almost all white, who had lived in the area for many years, but the area was also a place of refuge for people unable to obtain a settled home elsewhere. Most of the newer arrivals were living in run-down properties, where they had to share the use of bathrooms and toilets, paying high rents for insecure accommodation. Many families with young children were living in a single room.

To understand why and how this happened it is necessary to draw together some key events: the huge post-war slum clearance programme which had transformed the character of inner city areas; the effects of the 1957 Rent Act, which had removed security of tenure from many private tenants; and the arrival in Britain during the 1950s of a large number of newcomers, especially from the West Indies.

The post-war clearance programme
At the end of the Second World War Britain faced a major housing crisis. During the war almost half a million homes had been destroyed by bombing, and another half a million were very severely damaged. No new houses had been built since the beginning of the war. After years of being separated by the war, millions of families urgently wanted a new home where they could settle and bring up their children.

A major house-building programme was launched to replace the old slums and build new housing, with more than half the homes being built by local authorities, who became virtually the sole providers of new rented homes.

In the areas covered by the clearance programmes many tenants failed to get re-housed by the Council. Tenants who had moved into an area after the clearance plans had been decided by the Council were not deemed eligible for re-housing. Private landlords in clearance areas often evicted insecure tenants, in the hope they would get more money from the Council if the property was sold with vacant possession. Many local councils had a policy of not re-housing furnished tenants in clearance areas, because they were – often quite wrongly – considered to be transient. It was the newer arrivals, especially those who had come from the black, Commonwealth countries, who were most frequently excluded from re-housing into a secure new home.

As the need to re-house tenants from the areas to be cleared was given priority, fewer applicants from the local authority waiting list could be re-housed. As sharing and overcrowding got worse in the neighbourhoods not covered by the clearance programmes, so did the prospects of being re-housed by the Council. It was a vicious circle.

Tenants re-housed from the slums moved into flats on new estates, whilst many of those who could afford to moved to buy homes in suburban areas. But these opportunities by-passed new arrivals, who were deemed ineligible for re-housing because they had not lived long enough in the area.

Across swathes of inner London low income tenants were living in multi-occupied, poorly equipped and insecure flats, mostly rented from private landlords. North Kensington suffered from worse levels of overcrowding than any other area in the country, with thousands of families having only a single room for parents and their children. Many tenants had only limited security of tenure, and if they upset the landlord, for example by complaining that repairs were not being carried out, they faced being forced out on the streets.

A number of charitable housing associations had been set up in the Victorian era to provide low cost housing for working class tenants, notably the Peabody, Guinness, Samuel Lewis and William Sutton Trusts. The Octavia Hill and Rowe Housing Trust were two small associations formed shortly after the turn of the century in Notting Hill.

In the post war period the generally accepted view was that only local authorities were able to tackle the housing problems that existed. Housing associations received practically no help in public subsidy, and were seen as too small to tackle the scale of the housing task.

The 1957 Rent Act

The 1957 Rent Act ended controls on new lettings by private landlords. Existing tenants were still protected, but there were no limits to the rents landlords could charge on new lettings and tenants had no security against eviction.

In the areas of greatest housing pressure, such as North Kensington, landlords were able to charge high rents to those seeking somewhere to live. Some of the worst abuses were in Paddington and North Kensington, where tenants suffered harassment and illegal eviction by Peter Rachman and other private landlords. The worst actually sent round paid thugs to threaten tenants who complained about repairs or fell behind with their rent. Many tenants lived in constant fear. Most vulnerable were those such as older women living on their own.

Local advice centres and tenants organisations had been documenting the abuse for several years. Ben Parkin, the tireless Labour MP for Paddington, had been badgering ministers with Parliamentary Questions. However, it was only when Rachman was linked to Christine Keeler, in the revelations about her relationship with the Minister for War, John Profumo, that Rachman's activities as a landlord became front-page news.

Shocked into action by the revelations and the public outcry, the Prime Minister, Harold Macmillan, set up a high level inquiry into London's housing, under the chairmanship of Sir Milner Holland. The report was published in March 1965 and provided a powerful and authoritative picture of the scale and severity of London's housing problems, especially in the "twilight" areas of the inner city

By the time it was published a Labour Government had been elected and Harold Wilson was Prime Minister. One of the first actions of the Government was the emergency Protection Against Eviction Act, brought in to stop the practices of Rachman and other unscrupulous landlords. It was followed in 1965 by the Rent Act, which restored security of tenure to unfurnished tenants and prevented landlords charging more than the "fair rent" set by an independent Rent Officer. However, the Act did not cover furnished tenancies. Landlords who did not want their tenants to have security of tenure were able to let new tenancies as furnished, rather than unfurnished.

The arrival of new immigrants to Britain

In the decade after the "The Empire Windrush", the first ship carrying immigrants from the West Indies, sailed into Tilbury in 1948, tens of thousands of new settlers followed, attracted by advertisements for jobs, such as those on the buses or the underground, which paid higher wages than could be earned in their home islands.

One of the main areas they came to was Notting Hill, where it was possible to obtain privately rented accommodation, although it was mostly only furnished bedsits in multi-occupied houses. They did not anticipate the racial discrimination they would face, nor the dreadful housing conditions experienced by both black and white residents.

Initially there was little overt violence, but from 1956 onwards there were more signs of fascist groups trying to fan racial hostility. In April 1958 a crowd of 700 formed to protest at black immigration into the area.

The racial violence that many people feared erupted early one evening in May 1959. A young black man, Kelso Cochrane, was stabbed to death in Golborne Road in the heart of North Kensington. His murder sent shock waves, not only through the community where he had lived, but far beyond. It dramatically heightened concern over the fragile state of race relations in Britain's inner cities, and set off a train of events which would make Notting Hill a very different place to live in the years to come.

When the General Election was called for 8th October 1959, Sir Oswald Mosley, jailed during World War II for his fascistic Blackshirt activities, now leader of the National Front Party, announced that he would stand as a candidate in the Kensington constituency. He made it clear that he would campaign on the race issue. In David Butler's and Richard Rose's authoritative book on the 1959 General Election, Keith Kyle wrote a chapter on the North Kensington constituency, including a report of a speech of Mosley's.

"On a higher level he advocated compulsory free passage back to the West Indies for the immigrants, combined with heavy British investment to build up local West Indian employment and the purchase of British sugar from Jamaica. The low road led through long sordid tales of sexual offences by coloured men, spiced with such nasty remarks as that West Indians provided cheap labour because they could, at a pinch, live off a tin of Kit-E-Kat a day. These were the arguments of a British demagogue in the accents of a British gentleman".

The sitting Member of Parliament was George Rogers, the Labour Whip for London. A former railway clerk he had represented the constituency since 1945. To many people concerned about race relations, his response to the riots was dangerously equivocal. After a visit to the Home Office he had been reported as saying that the riots *"were the reaction of people very sorely tried by the behaviour of the West Indians"*. His views were repudiated by a number of leading Labour Party members in the constituency.

Some Labour supporters, led by Donald Chesworth, the Labour member for Kensington on the London County Council, were very critical of George Rogers and his failure to speak out against the racism of Mosley's campaign. To demonstrate the Labour Party's opposition to racism, they identified four hundred black and ethnic minority voters from the electoral register and circulated them with a statement from the Labour Party leader, Hugh Gaitskell, attacking all forms of racial discrimination.

When the count was taken George Rogers was re-elected, although with a slightly larger swing against him than the London average. Sir Oswald Mosley lost his deposit.

Kelso Cochrane's murder and the events of the General Election made many West Indians in Notting Hill more conscious of the racial hostility they faced, and apprehensive about their future. In his book "Notting Hill in the Sixties", the black writer, Mike Phillips, gives a graphic account of the funeral procession for Kelso Cochrane.

"It was a warm day and the sun was shining out of a sparkling blue sky. This seemed right because this was a unique Caribbean occasion, one of the biggest funerals ever seen in North Kensington. About 1200 people were walking in the procession, and more of them were lining the streets on the way to Kensal Green cemetery. But the man they were burying wasn't someone that most of them knew or cared about when he was alive. He was a thirty-three year old Jamaican carpenter named Kelso Cochrane, born for obscurity in the way of such people, except that one night in May he'd been stabbed to death by a group of whites out for blood.

In between the night of his bleeding to death on the pavement and the morning of the service at St. Michael's in Ladbroke Grove, he had become a martyr. The West Indians and their supporters were making the ceremony a state funeral, a demonstration which would leave an indelible mark on the area and its people, and speak to everyone who saw it about their identity and their determination to stay put".[1]

---

1. Michael Phillips, Notting Hill in the 1960s, 1969.

Chapter 2

THE EARLY YEARS

A response to the racial disturbances in Notting Hill, and the murder of Kelso Cochrane, came from an initiative by the Methodist Church. At its Annual Conference in 1960 there was a powerful appeal for the Church to have a stronger presence in deprived, inner city neighbourhoods, where too often it seemed to be almost invisible.

As a result, a team ministry was set up two years later, based in the Notting Hill Methodist Church, under the care of Rev. Donald Soper, the well-known and outspoken Superintendent of the West London Mission. The three new ministers, Norwyn Denny, David Mason and Geoffrey Ainger had a radical vision of how the church should express its presence in an outward-looking and inclusive way.

During the next decade the work of the church in Notting Hill was transformed, attracting many new members, especially from the Afro-Caribbean community and young professionals who had come to live in the area. It developed innovative forms of worship and extended its activities in the local community. It achieved widespread recognition as an example of successful renewal of the church in a multi-racial, inner city area.

One of the first actions of the team ministry was to set up the Notting Hill Social Council, chaired by David Mason. This brought together a wide range of voluntary organisations, and sought to use its position representing respected community organisations to convey its views for improving social conditions to the Borough Council.

Members of the Social Council saw the housing problems in North Kensington as a major priority. Two hundred signatures were obtained from representatives of different organisations for a petition to the Borough Council, urging it to buy up empty properties and to let them at reasonable rents to families with young children. The petition was ignored.

The lack of response was a setback to members of the Social Council, and reinforced fears that the local authority was unwilling to tackle the housing problems in Notting Hill with the urgency they believed was needed.

The arrival of Bruce Kenrick

A new associate member of the Methodist Group Ministry to come to Notting Hill in 1962 was Rev. Bruce Kenrick, a Minister of the Church of Scotland. Some years earlier he had met one of the future members of the Group Ministry, Rev. Geoffrey Ainger, at a World Council of Churches summer course and they had maintained their friendship. As a result, he was invited to come to Notting Hill and join the Group Ministry.

Bruce Kenrick had served during the war in the Army Medical Corps in Africa and Italy. When the war ended he continued his medical studies, but then enrolled at the theological faculty of Edinburgh University after deciding that his vocation was as a minister. During this time he had met his future wife, Isabel. They married in 1954 and spent the next nine months working in East Harlem in New York.

The following year they went to Calcutta in India, with the aim of spending the rest of their lives there as Church of Scotland missionaries. However, whilst in India Bruce contracted a severe bout of typhoid and became very seriously ill. As he got weaker and weaker the couple decided to return to England, where his GP discovered that his illness was the result of inadequate treatment for typhoid. The only cure would be long-term rest and recuperation. For three years he convalesced on the island of Iona, with his wife and their three young children, camping during the summer and renting a small cottage in the winter.

During his convalescence Bruce wrote "Come out the Wilderness", which told the story of how the ecumenical East Harlem Protestant parish had brought poor and disadvantaged residents into its storefront worship and activities, and also became deeply engaged in social and political action, challenging corrupt local government and campaigning for better housing and education. The book was widely sold in both the United States and England, and became the "religious book of the month" in the United States.

When the Kenricks arrived in Notting Hill they found a home at 115, Blenheim Crescent, a four storied terrace house. which they were able to buy with a legacy from Bruce's father. When the family moved in there was no kitchen, no bathroom, and for heating only a coal fire or paraffin stove. The back wall was collapsing and during the first winter the roof leaked badly.

When Bruce Kenrick came to Notting Hill he was appalled by the housing conditions in which people were living, especially families with young children. Bruce wrote later:

"What struck me painfully about Notting Hill was the extent to which people's problems stemmed from damnable housing conditions. Marriages broke up because one

or other partner could no longer stand the strain of living in one room, with a stove and a sink squeezed into one corner, and the washing dripping from a clothes-line above on to the crumbling lino." [1]

The Social Council was lobbying the Council to increase its housing activities in North Kensington, both by acquiring and renovating properties and building new homes. Bruce Kenrick, however, believed that they could not wait for the Council to act and that *"we must buy scores of houses now, and convert them into good simple flats, let at reasonable rents to those in need"*.

So he and his wife brought together a small group of people to form a new housing association. At its first meeting on 18 December 1963 Bruce Kenrick asked the Committee to consider three aims that he outlined in a paper called "Project Notting Hill":

> *"1. Pilot: To buy and convert three houses in Notting Hill*
> *2. Major: To buy local houses on largest possible scale*
> *3. To launch similar work in other needy cities throughout the UK".*

Whilst the immediate aim was to buy a small number of properties in Notting Hill, the paper clearly shows that even at this early stage Bruce Kenrick wanted to expand the work to other cities.

It would have been possible for him and his colleagues to offer to work with the charitable housing associations already active in the area, rather than to set up a new association. The Kensington Housing Trust was doing more or less exactly the sort of work that Bruce Kenrick and his colleagues proposed for their new housing association. However little of this existing activity in helping families threatened with homelessness was known to those who set up the Notting Hill Trust.

The existing housing associations in North Kensington were seen as very conservative organisations. The Kensington Housing Trust in particular was viewed with suspicion by some community organisations in North Kensington because of its close links with Conservative members of the Borough Council. Bruce Kenrick saw the Notting Hill Housing Trust as something different - a crusade for tackling poor housing.

The first activity of the Trust was modest, a fundraising stall in Portobello Road, which raised £24. Shortly after, however, it received a much larger donation: £7,000 from the Christian Action's Homeless in Britain Fund, who had agreed to run a national appeal to raise money for the Trust. The first instalment was used to buy the first house, at 107 Blenheim Crescent, only a few doors away from where the Kenricks lived.

Soon afterwards Bruce Kenrick received an offer of an interest free loan of £7,000 for 10 years. He asked the donor if the money could be used for a national advertising campaign to raise money for the Trust, and received the answer: *"Do what you like with it"*.

An executive in an advertising agency offered the Trust his firm's help with press advertising without charge. The campaign was launched with advertisements 12 inches high and 4 columns wide in the national and religious press. The first advertisement was a test in the Guardian.

Below a large photo of an overcrowded family was the bold black headline:

HEARTBREAK NOTTING HILL AND YOU

Expectant mother, father and two children made their home in the basement room above. It measures 10 feet by 10 feet. The toilet is shared by 24 people. Rain comes in through the Window. Rats are present. If this doesn't make your blood boil read no further.....

Right here in the heart of Britain there are hundreds of families living in the same sub-human squalor.... The Notting Hill Housing Trust is taking action. The slums of Notting Hill are immoral, a blot on the conscience of us all. Please help us wipe them out and make Britain a happier, safer place.

The appeal absorbed the entire loan, but raised £20,000, and also provided a mailing list for recruiting regular donors in the future.

An example of the enthusiastic local response to the Trust's appeals for money came at a wealthy church not far from Notting Hill. One Sunday evensong, the vicar told his congregation that it cost the Trust £325 to house a homeless family. He said he wanted that evening's offering to raise £325, by notes, cheques or IOU's. The collection was taken, counted and found to total only £253. *"Lock the doors. We'll take another collection"*, said the vicar. This was done. Later a smiling vicar announced *"It's £425. Open the doors"*.

In the early years of the Trust Bruce Kenrick used his exceptional powers of persuasion to secure appearances on prime time television, as well as radio broadcasts to promote the work of the Trust and appeal for urgently needed money. One early example was the Sunday Break programme at Christmas 1963.

No housing association had previously appealed for support in this way. Its impact was not only the money it raised, but also the powerful and shocking message about the housing conditions in Notting Hill. Within months the fledgling Trust had acquired a national reputation,

Locally the Trust was strengthening its Committee with members from local community organisations. Among the initial members was Pansy Jeffrey, who was a staff member at the local Citizen's Advice Bureau and had daily knowledge of the housing difficulties experienced by local residents. She was also an active member of the Social Council and her views were often sought as one of the best known West Indians working in the area.

Another key member of the Committee was Sidney Miller, the Manager of the Family Service Unit who became Vice Chairman of the Trust. In his 50s, he was a gaunt man, a familiar figure cycling round the streets of Notting Hill. He had a deep knowledge of life in the area drawn from many years experience of working with low income, vulnerable families and seeing the hardship caused by the housing conditions.

He played a key role in drawing up the Trust's policies on the rents that should be charged for different sizes of accommodation and the allocations policy for deciding which of the hundreds of applicants should be given priority for newly converted flats. His knowledge of the local community, passionate social concern and ability to apply this in practical decision-making, were immensely important.

In October 1962 the Family Service Unit had carried out a survey of estate agents and local newspaper advertisements across London, which showed the virtual impossibility of finding unfurnished flats at rents low income families could afford. Following the 1957 Rent Act most landlords were only letting furnished accommodation, where the rents were higher and tenants had no security.

Another person who has played an important role in the work of the Trust for many years is Anthony Taussig. His first action to help the Trust was as the "anonymous donor" whose interest free loan of £7,000 – later made into a gift - enabled the Trust to launch its first national advertising campaign. He had recently come to live in London and was shocked by the appalling housing conditions he saw. Having heard about the work of the Trust he wrote to Bruce Kenrick and shortly afterwards went to meet him to discuss how he might help.

He joined the Trust's Finance Advisory Committee in 1964 and became a member of the full Committee three years later. He was the Chair of the Trust from 1988 to 1994 and remained a Committee member until 2004. Over this time he was also a tireless member of the Trust's sub-committees and subsidiary companies, renowned for his commitment and vigilance.

The day to day work of the Trust

The Trust started buying vacant properties to convert them into family flats, and let them to families from the most overcrowded flats. In the first year 5 houses were bought, which after conversion provided accommodation for 58 people. The Committee agreed a target of acquiring 25 more houses in the second year, but only 17 were acquired. For the third year the target was 70 houses.

In March 1965 Sir Milner Holland's report on Greater London housing was published and made news in every national newspaper. It provided a powerful and authoritative picture of the scale and severity of London housing problems, especially in the "twilight" areas of the inner city, and the way Rachman had made the lives of his tenants almost unbearable misery.

Given notice of its publication the Trust booked advertising space in the local press to appear on the same pages as coverage of the report. For seven days offers of help poured into the Trust's office, gifts reached almost £10,000. Shortly afterwards Sir Milner Holland agreed to address the Trust's first AGM.

The report of the Milner Holland committee was critical of the older housing associations for not having built more homes in the years since the war. It expressed doubts on whether housing associations had the capacity to play a leading role in meeting the desperate housing shortage in London. The Notting Hill Housing Trust faced an uphill battle if it was to gain the political support and public credibility it sought.

Addressing the AGM, Sir Milner Holland said, *"I'm delighted that, at the end of the first year you have £300,000 worth of homes in the pipeline. And I'm equally delighted you believe that politics is the final answer to bad housing. But until that political answer is fully given, there's nothing better that the private citizen can do than engage in work like yours."*

From its earliest days the Trust was innovative. In its first year, for example, agreement was reached with a local authority in the North East to accept four families for re-housing, who moved to new homes in that area. The following year the Trust supported the creation of a new housing association, Nelson and Colne, which would take families from Notting Hill. This could be seen as an early forerunner of later initiatives to enable people to move to homes and jobs in areas of lower demand.

Much of the initial work of Bruce Kenrick and the small group of supporters was to raise money, since without this the rents would have been too high for low income households. In effect the money raised from donations was used as a capital subsidy.

When the Trust was launched nobody had a clear idea of where the money would come from to meet all the costs of purchase and conversion. The initial idea was to use the money raised by the advertising appeals, but relying on this alone would make buying properties painfully slow. One idea was that a lot of the work could be done by volunteers, but this greatly under-estimated how much building work was needed.

However, an encouraging meeting with the London County Council early in 1964 opened up an important source of funding. As well as officers from the LCC, this meeting was attended by Donald Chesworth, the Labour LCC member for North Kensington, who had led the criticism of George Rogers for his failure to challenge more strongly the racism of Sir Oswald Mosley. He had also been a member of the action group set up to expose the activities of Rachman in the early 1960s and was passionately committed to tackling housing problems in the area.

The Trust delegation was encouraged by the LCC's response. It offered to give 90% mortgages for buying houses. The Trust used money from donations to pay the remaining 10%. At the time, the average cost of purchasing a property and carrying out essential repairs to create a self-contained flat was £3,250, so the charitable element needed was £325. This became the basis of the appeal for donations: *"Give us £325 and we will house a family"*.

The work of acquisition, rehabilitation, lettings and housing management was obviously also essential, and proved to be more complex and difficult than had been foreseen at the start. The decision to appoint a Housing Manager was a very important step. The Trust was fortunate in recruiting an experienced and qualified housing professional, John Coward, who was appointed in March 1965.

John Coward had left the army in 1947, and had worked for seventeen years in local government housing departments. When he responded to the Trust's advertisement he was the deputy housing manager for the Borough of Richmond, but he had previously worked as a housing officer in Kensington. He applied because of the frustration and boredom he felt at the unchanging routine of council bureaucracy, but he knew he was taking a huge risk. His friends and family advised against it. His father was horrified that he was abandoning a secure local authority job and the prospect of a good pension.

When he joined the Trust he was 42 years old, a tall, quietly-mannered, bespectacled man. He had solid experience of local authority housing management, but none of the very different challenges facing the fledgling housing association. Although the title of the post was Housing Manager – it was not changed to Director until some years later - the responsibilities included every aspect of the Trust's work apart from fundraising. The way he mastered the skills required was to have enormous significance for the Trust as it moved from the enthusiastic amateurism of its early days to become a respected and professional housing organisation.

The office John moved in to was a ground floor room in a four storey terraced house at 107 Blenheim Crescent, which the Trust had just bought. The floors above were occupied by families waiting for re-housing into newly converted flats. The only other person working in the office was the volunteer who collected the rents, recording them in a Woolworth's notebook. The fundraising and publicity activity was carried out from the Kenricks' house further down Blenheim Crescent.

The task of buying up and renovating individual houses was very different from managing purpose-built council estates. Few of the properties had experienced comprehensive renovation since they were built in the mid nineteenth century. Initially many had been occupied as large family houses, but as those residents had moved away to suburban areas, the properties had been divided into multi-occupied lettings, with tenants sharing bathrooms, toilets and kitchens.

Many had been badly neglected by the landlords for years, and suffered from the wear and tear caused by high levels of sharing and overcrowding. Leaking roofs, rotting windows, defective electrical wiring and rising damp were common problems. Rectifying the disrepair and converting the properties into properly equipped, self-contained flats was a complex and expensive task. It was especially difficult to provide three or four bedroom flats for larger families. Yet these were the people in the greatest need.

An important breakthrough came early in 1967 when Bruce Kenrick had dinner with Anthony Greenwood, the Labour Housing Minister. He put to the Minister the difficulties being faced by associations in buying and converting older properties. The Trust's files contain John Coward's handwritten notes with calculations of what this meant for a sample of properties in the areas where it was working. The problem was that local authorities and housing associations could get subsidies for building new homes, but these were not available for converting existing properties.

Bruce wrote immediately to the Minister, using a briefing note prepared by John Coward. After thanking him for an *"enjoyable evening – and a delicious dinner"*, his letter spelt out the extra financial help the Trust needed for buying and rehabilitating older properties. At the time it was borrowing at 7%. It was calculated that an interest rate of no more than 4% could be afforded to finance the costs of management, maintenance and loan charges (for interest and capital repayments).

The letter concluded:

"At well under £500 per person the conversion of existing properties is much cheaper than new building – and they will last at least 30 years. The capital will be repaid twice as fast as repayments for new building over 60 years. And damn it (if I may use a biblical expression) homeless people will be housed much faster.

To summarize: The housing itself is cheaper.
The Treasury gets it cash back twice as fast.
Cathys in costly hostels get out faster.
The drain on the Treasury is plugged".

The reply from Anthony Greenwood could scarcely have been more encouraging. The Minister announced that the Government would make amendments to the Housing Subsidies Bill going through Parliament *"to pay grants on both acquisition and works in the case of properties acquired and improved or converted by housing associations".*

There would be a new grant to cover three-eighths of the loan charges. This would achieve what the Trust was asking by reducing the interest rate from 7% to 4%, and would make the subsidy the same as that given to housing associations and local authorities for new building.

By 1969, the Trust was able in most instances to borrow 100% mortgages from local authorities, without needing to use its charitable money to make up the difference between a mortgage of 80% or 90% and the cost of buying and converting the property. The drawback of this was that the rents charged, even after the new higher subsidies, were often beyond the means of the tenants the Trust was re-housing. It had to use its charitable funds to finance a rebate scheme to help those tenants.

The work of renovating the houses was a slow and frustrating job. Finance had to be found to pay for the cost of conversion, including arranging loans, securing approval for improvement grants from the local authority and topping these up with the charitable money raised by the Trust itself. It meant appointing external surveyors to draw up specifications, yet there were frequently difficulties because they lacked experience in this type of work. Planning consent had to be obtained from the local authority. Work could only start when other newly converted flats were ready for sitting tenants to move in to.

Almost invariably unforeseen problems were discovered whilst building work was in progress, and funding had to be found to meet the excess costs. An important step was the appointment of Ray Hunter as a consultant surveyor for houses the Trust was buying. When John Coward met him he was working on his own from an office in Esher. He quickly brought much needed systems to each stage of the renovation process, agreeing standard project briefs, space and design standards and procedures for approving cost-overruns, so that Trust staff were able to issue straightforward instructions and approvals at every stage of the process.

The Trust quickly outgrew the small office in Blenheim Crescent, and was under strong pressure from the Borough Council to move as the property did not have planning permission for office use. In 1969 it moved to new offices in All Saints Road, where it had developed ground floor offices and 21 flats, on a derelict site previously occupied by the Ridgways laundry.

Moving to All Saints Road was a significant move. It placed the Trust offices right in the heart of its chosen area in North Kensington. The Mangrove, the very popular Afro-Caribbean restaurant, was in the same street, which was thronged every day with people using the shops and walking up and down.

The staff of the Trust

The work of the Trust grew rapidly, with higher targets being set each year for buying and renovating houses. As the programme grew, more staff were appointed. Most came with no previous experience in housing, but attracted by the challenges of tackling the desperate housing problems in Notting Hill.

One of the new staff was Dudley Savill, who was interviewed by Bruce Kenrick in January 1966. At the time he was 30 years old and had previously worked with the United Nations Association organising volunteers for development projects in Greece, and then as the personal assistant to Cecil Jackson-Coles, the redoubtable founder of Help the Aged.

After the interview Bruce wrote to Dudley offering him a job and describing how he saw the post. After setting out the tasks of visiting tenants in their homes, advising on any problems they faced and interviewing prospective tenants, the letter went on:

"In the context of your growing knowledge of the families, you will be able to select those who might benefit from moving to a new job and a new home in the north; those who might make the greatest contribution to our experiment in racial integration, and those who might improve their lot by taking advantage of a Government training centre. All of which will obviously take a great deal of time and an enormous amount of patience; the depth of which it could – and will – provide a completely fresh start in life for hundreds of families is, in my view, unfathomable. The work will be immensely demanding and, I believe, immensely rewarding".

The letter is illuminating. It shows Bruce's ambitious vision of how he saw the Trust not only putting roofs over people's heads but also helping them to achieve dramatic changes to their lives, whether through training for employment, moving to a new area of the country or contributing to racial integration.

In November 1965 Bruce wrote an article "Homeless near a Thousand Homes" about the work of the Trust for the ecumenical New Christian magazine:

"We make no secret of the fact that we see the Trust as a fragment of the church. A fragment whose dynamic is enshrined in the sacrament we celebrate together. Each second Wednesday at noon all who work full-time in the Trust – housing manager, secretary, typists, director, foreman – meet in a Notting Hill home around the table".

In his letter to Dudley he described how he saw the Trust:

"As an experiment aimed at discovering new ways in which the non-institutional church could be relevant and creative. One of the reasons for my pleasure at the fact that you are joining our team is the knowledge that you too are eager to discover patterns through which the essentials of the faith can have a formative effect on the so-called "ordinary" structures of everyday life. We are helped as a team to remember the dynamic at the heart of our work by our fortnightly celebration of the sacrament in a very simple form before having lunch together in my home".

Dudley remembers: *"Those lunches every two weeks where all the staff would come together, and we could take the sacrament if we wanted to, and then we would talk about the housing and the problems and the drains and whatever else. They were wonderful, wonderful events, absolutely fascinating because there you saw Bruce at his very best".*

Almost inevitably, however, these lunchtime meetings lapsed as the Trust expanded and staff were recruited who did not share the same Christian faith. There continued to be a number of staff members who had joined the Trust as a result of their Christian commitment, but the Trust itself developed as a secular organisation, where people of different religious beliefs, and none, worked together.

Dudley found that his work had a regular weekly pattern. From Monday to Wednesday he went round visiting tenants in their homes and discussing any difficulties they were experiencing. A lot of these were with paying the rent, or having the money for electricity meters. Although the Trust tried to keep the rents low, there was no housing benefit system for tenants on low wages. On Thursday his job was to visit people who had applied for housing, and write a report on all the circumstances and present this to Sidney Miller. Dudley recalls how desperate the conditions were, for example two parents and four children having to share a single room. Making a choice of who to house needed *"the judgement of Solomon"*.

On his visits Dudley used to collect rent from tenants. On one occasion he was attacked by two young men as he approached his car in a street near Shepherd's Bush with a bag holding £350. He was pushed to the ground, but clung desperately to the bag of money, despite being kicked as he lay there. A number of people gathered, but none came to his help until an elderly lady strode up, brought her umbrella down sharply on the heads of the two assailants and they ran off. What they did not know was that Dudley was a well-known amateur boxer. He recalls that he might have been tempted to use his skills if he had not been so determined to cling on to the rent.

Sam Hood joined the Trust in 1968. He had read Bruce Kenrick's book "Come out the Wilderness", and invited him to come and speak to the Student Christian Movement group he ran at the secondary school where he was teaching. Unfortunately Bruce was not able to do so because of illness, but Dudley Savill went instead and enthused his audience by his description of the Trust's work. As a result Sam brought groups of students to do voluntary work at the weekend. After several visits he asked about the possibility of a job with the Trust.

He recalls John Coward offering him a post as a student housing manager, provided he enrolled for the Institute of Housing course to qualify as a professional housing manager. The salary would be £850 a year, which was half what he was earning as a qualified teacher. Sam thought hard, but knew it was what he really wanted to do, and accepted the job. He stayed eight years, becoming in turn Housing Manager and then Deputy Director.

All those who worked with the Trust in these early years recall the strong "buzz" of creativity and breaking new ground. The excitement came in part from being in close day-to-day contact with the community, working to find solutions to the acute and complex difficulties which people were experiencing. Responsibility was delegated. Staff were encouraged to be innovative. All this encouraged a very high level of commitment and enthusiasm.

Sam Hood recalls one occasion when he went to an auction hoping to buy four houses in Westbourne Park Road occupied by furnished tenants who risked being evicted and becoming homeless if the Trust could not buy. At that time acquiring properties was becoming difficult because house prices were rising very rapidly, and the Trust was becoming worried about the effects on its development programme.

The District Valuer, whose job it was to assess the market value of any house the association wanted to buy, had put a price ceiling of £50,000 for the properties. However, the bidding quickly went over that amount. Determined not to lose the properties, Sam Hood continued to bid, desperately thinking *"I can't let it go, I can't let it go"*, and in the end triumphantly bought the lot for £72,000.

He went back to the Trust offices pleased with his success, until John Coward raised the question of how the Trust would pay for the houses. There was a firm rule that no offer should be made above the Valuer's ceiling. In addition, under the rules of buying at an auction the successful bidder must complete within 28 days.

Fortunately, a plan of action was worked out. The Trust's accountant, Martin Prater, persuaded the bank manager to provide bridging finance by arguing that if he accepted the security of holding the title deeds of the house he had a sound investment. And after long negotiations the Council officers were persuaded that the price paid must have been the true market price, since it was the lowest amount the property could be bought for at a competitive auction.

Sam Hood remembers it today as a *"terrible mistake"*, which might have lost him his job. Others recall it as an example of the determination which fired staff to do everything they could to house more people.

Notting Hill was an area of very severe deprivation. Tenants living in cramped, squalid conditions, with no way of finding anywhere better, felt a great despair hanging over them. Mothers with young children lived with the daily misery of having to share toilets and bathrooms, even kitchens. Black people experienced racial hostility and discrimination.

Many of the tenants housed by the Trust needed help with a wide range of problems. These ranged from problems of loneliness and isolation to severe poverty which made them unable to provide furniture, curtains or floor-coverings when moving from a furnished to an unfurnished flat.

The staff were very conscious of being "in the front line", at the same time as coping with the pressures from people who were desperate to get a flat from the Trust, they were doing all they could to keep increasing the supply of properties. Although they had the satisfaction of knowing the value of what they were doing, they had to cope with the pent-up anger of people who came into the office, including verbal abuse and at times threats of physical violence.

In order to respond to these needs, the Trust employed a qualified social worker, Hilary Darton, to help vulnerable tenants and she built up a team of trained volunteers who assisted in this work. She became expert at identifying charitable trusts who might make donations to help needy tenants and was very successful in the applications she made.

In spite of the pressures, a number of staff stayed with the Trust for many years. Martin Prater joined the Trust as its first Accountant in 1969. He had been working with a city firm of accountants, but was becoming frustrated in his job and looking for an opportunity to work with a charity. He had grown up in a strongly Methodist family and was the secretary of the Council of Churches in Gravesend, where he and his wife lived. Through the Council he had helped to set up the Gravesend Churches Housing Association, and become its Treasurer.

He vividly recalls coming for an interview at the Trust's new offices in All Saints Road, which were looking like a building site because the work was some way from being complete. Before he arrived the financial work had been done by the bookkeeper and the voluntary Treasurer, Michael Jacob, who was a senior manager with Land Securities. All the entries had been done by hand and there had been no practice of preparing annual budgets.

Martin stayed with the Trust until retiring in 1999, with his role changing to become Financial Director, then Deputy Director and finally working part-time prior to his retirement as Internal Auditor.

Pat Gaudin (later White) had come to live in Notting Hill after several years working as a journalist on the provincial and national press. Having been introduced to the Trust by a friend, David Wilcox, who was then the planning correspondent with the Evening Standard, she went to the Trust offices to meet John Coward and *"was absolutely bowled over by what those people were doing"*.

John Coward offered her a job, and her main role initially was as the press officer and advising John Coward on public relations. The Trust had been having a hard time with the local press, who were regularly reporting negative stories, for example about squatters who were being evicted and about people whose expectations had been raised by seeing local houses converted, but who could not get re-housed by the Trust. The waiting list of people in severe housing need was still very long, and at times had to be closed to new applicants.

Pat recalls finding the task of improving the Trust's image was surprisingly straightforward. She simply made direct contact with local reporters and fed them positive stories about what the Trust was actually doing. *"Because there was such integrity in the organisation it made it easy to deal with its public face"* she says.

The success of the Trust in attracting able staff is shown by the number recruited in the early years who went on to hold senior posts in other major housing associations. Sam Hood became Chief Executive of the Samuel Lewis Trust, and later the Knightstone Housing Group; Peter Naish became the Chief Executive of Salford Family Housing Association, then of English Churches Housing Group and also Chair of the NFHA; Roger Tuson became Chief Executive of North Cheshire Housing Association; Andrew Williamson became the Chief Executive of Hastoe Housing Association.

The same happened to a number of staff who worked with the Trust in the 1980s and early 90s. Geoff Murray became Chief Executive of Kensington Housing Trust; Adrian Norridge became Chief Executive of the

St. Pancras Housing Trust; Simon Dow became a Deputy Chief Executive of the Housing Corporation, and then Chief Executive of the Guinness Trust; Andrew Wiles became South West Director of the Housing Corporation; Steve Howlett was appointed Chief Executive of the Peabody Trust.

The Chair of the Trust

A vital mainstay of the Trust for many years was Sir Roger Ormrod, later Lord Justice Ormrod, a High Court and then Court of Appeal judge, who took over as the Chair in 1968. He was a resident of Kensington, living close to Holland Park. As a judge he had been responsible for the landmark decision which entitled women to 50% of the joint possessions when two married people divorced. John Coward stressed how much he valued the support he was given as Director by Roger Ormrod. *"He was always available for advice when asked, willing whenever needed to come to meetings with tenants and absolutely committed to the work of the Trust"*. Pat White described his *"quiet strength"*. He seemed *"like a grown up, someone of real integrity"*.

A tribute given at the memorial service after his death in 1992 summarised his qualities:

"In 1968 Roger Ormrod agreed to become the Chairman of the Notting Hill Housing Trust which had been formed a few years earlier to provide decent homes for people living the area to the north of his house in Aubrey Road (close to Notting Hill Gate).

The Trust's campaign enjoyed considerable success. But success ushered in difficulties for an inexperienced organisation. The rapid growth and the volume and visibility of the Trust's work made it the object of some political controversy. There could have been few people with greater ability to provide the unquestioned stature, experience and political neutrality around whom, and through whom, the internal and external pressures could be contained and met".

Pat Gaudin's future husband, Michael White, now the Political Editor of the Guardian, was then a reporter on the London Evening Standard. He also helped the Trust by writing fundraising leaflets and newsletters. Later he became a member of the North Kensington Area Committee and the full Committee of Management, but was by then working nightshifts on the Guardian and, in his own words, was not *"a cutting edge"* member of the Committee. However, he has known John Coward and the Trust's work since those early days.

Michael recalls going to The Pelican pub in All Saints Rd with John one evening where they struck up a conversation with the writer, Colin MacInness. He had written "Absolute Beginners", a widely admired novel about Notting Hill and the "new" London of the Sixties a few years earlier and wanted to impress his companions with his significance. John was characteristically modest about his own achievements in the community and allowed the writer to patronise him. As a "punishment" for his insensitivity to the heroic John Coward Michael pretended never to have heard of MacInness, to the writer's increasing frustration. Meanwhile John sat quietly by, oblivious to the battle of egos.

"John was an enabler. He was modest, in many ways innocent, yet able to persuade people more readily than very egotistical characters often do. For me the vindication of what the Trust had done came when the riots took place in other inner city areas in 1981. North Kensington did not burn".

Taking stock

At the end of 1968 the Trust was five years old. It had grown from a small group of people meeting in the Kenricks' house into an established and dynamic organisation. It was well known in North Kensington. As a result of powerful fundraising appeals its work was also known nationally. Without doubt it was the best known of the new, 1960s generation of housing associations.

In 1969, the Trust owned 137 houses, which would provide 442 homes when all the renovation work was completed. From starting with nothing five years before this was an impressive achievement. Yet all the hard work had scarcely made a dent in the housing problems. Rising prices were making it increasingly difficult for the Trust to buy properties in North Kensington as potentially handsome Victorian houses in the area were restored to their former glory in a process that was becoming known as gentrification.

The Annual Report showed fewer than thirty per cent of the Trust's properties were in W10 and W11, with the rest outside North Kensington. The rising tide of gentrification and the activities of the property speculators were threatening to force poorer tenants out of Notting Hill.

An outspoken challenge to the Trust to fight against this came in a special issue of the "Community Notebook", written by Ann Warden (later Holmes) and published by the Notting Hill Community Workshop in the autumn of 1968. Featuring a photograph of a house with the sign "Acquired by the Notting Hill Housing Trust", the magazine was a twenty page critique of the role that housing associations had played in North Kensington and the prospects for the future.

The early section reviewed the history of the older associations formed at the turn of the century: the Octavia Hill Trust, the Improved Tenements Association, the Rowe Housing Trust. They were followed in the 1920s and 30s by the formation of the Kensington Housing Trust and two large estates built by the Peabody Trust and the William Sutton Trust in the north west corner of the Borough.

Of the older housing associations only the Kensington Housing Trust (KHT) had sought to increase awareness of the housing problems in the borough, and to put pressure on the Council. This activity had taken place in the ten years after it was formed in 1926.

However, KHT had never publicly criticised the policies of the Council. Leading Conservative councillors held senior roles in the Trust, notably Lord Burleigh who was an influential member of the Council and KHT in the 20s and 30s. The Notebook ended with a searing indictment:

"In practice the Kensington Housing Trust has become the 'second arm' of the Council, taking on those jobs that the Council is unwilling to do, such as the re-housing of the homeless… The result was to take the stress out of what would otherwise have been an intolerable situation".

The Notebook recognizes the different character of the Notting Hill Housing Trust from the others in the borough, describing it as:

"The prototype of the 1960s 'model housing trust – the practical expression of the Shelter image'. In many ways it differs from the Octavia Hill model. It is less closely linked to the Council establishment, less paternalist in approach. It has hopes for tenant participation in management. It has given higher priority to the larger, and especially immigrant families.

But the essence of the policy is similar. Over their 5 year life their (the Notting Hill Housing Trust's) actions have been shaped to supplement, but not challenge the policies of local and national authorities. They do not interfere with the property market, since their purchases are backed by no power of compulsion, and owners can always sell to the highest bidder. Their reliance on the authorities for loans inevitably places the Trust in a dependent role. Although it is not their intention the Trust gives the impression that something is being done in areas of stagnating conditions, and so offers an excuse for the authorities who perpetuate the neglect."

The *Notebook* concludes by arguing that the housing trusts:

"which for nearly a century have insisted that decent secure housing is a first necessity for family life, will find themselves playing an increasing part in divisive, nationally supported housing policies. The question must be: Can they resist this as well as throwing off the remains of paternalism inherited from the past? This means that they must take their place in the movement to make Notting Hill a better place to live in - for those who live here now. It will mean a radical re-definition of their role.

The Trusts should place their knowledge, reputation and resources in a determined effort to prevent the erosion of cheap rented accommodation by a high income, middle class invasion. They should urge the Borough Council to use compulsory purchase powers to acquire property, especially to intervene in the open market to thwart speculators and to take over property where landlords will not or cannot carry out the work needed to make it habitable."

The views in the Notebook were those of the author and a small group of individuals from the Community Workshop. They were not necessarily shared by people in the wide range of organisations active in Notting Hill or by the tenants desperately wanting a solution to their housing problems. Yet members of the Workshop were active and influential in a number of organisations, especially the People's Association.

There is little doubt that many of those active in the area had reservations, if not stronger doubts, about the ability of housing associations to make a substantial difference. The collapse of Ronan Point – a high rise block of flats in Newham - in 1968 had triggered a dramatic loss of confidence in "mass housing", industrialised housing systems. Yet many people, especially Labour supporters and those with left-wing views, still believed that only local authorities could provide the scale of low cost rented homes that were needed in an area like Notting Hill. No political party was promising a large increase in support for housing associations.

1968 saw a total of 413,000 new homes built, the largest number in the UK since the war, with half of them built by local authorities. The number of new homes built by housing associations totalled just over 6,000, and many of those were in cost rent schemes too expensive for low income families.

The Milner Holland report had been sceptical about the contribution that housing associations could make. Sir Milner Holland had spoken warmly about the work of the Trust at the AGM in 1965, but had seen voluntary bodies as providing only emergency help until the time when the state would inject adequate resources.

With the shocking report of a major housing survey carried out in Notting Hill about to be published, the Council was shortly to come under intense pressure to use its housing powers more strongly in North Kensington. By virtue of being given the lead role in the Colville/Tavistock area, the Trust would be placed in the front-line in the struggle to defeat the gentrifying property speculators and buy houses for local tenants.

Within the next few years the Trust would play an important role in developing a new approach to area-based housing renewal, shaping a new subsidy system for housing associations, and significantly changing the balance of power in the National Federation of Housing Associations.

At the end of 1968, however, only a supreme optimist would have foreseen the transformation in the Trust's standing and future prospects that would take place over the coming five years. Fortunately within the Trust, optimism was one commodity not in short supply.

---

1. *New Christian, November 1965.*

Chapter 3

MAKING ITS MARK

In the years between 1969 and 1973 the Trust continued to grow rapidly. The Annual Reports, which had been short duplicated documents for the first three years of the Trust's existence, grew longer in the following years as they reported a widening number of activities. They were produced in a plain format and gave quite detailed accounts of developments in the year.

The tenants fortunate to be re-housed by the Trust were delighted that they had been able to escape from the living conditions they had experienced. Yet many more people in the area were still living in overcrowded, run down properties, forced to share bathrooms and toilets, and often kitchens too, paying high rents and with little security against evictions.

The Trust was seen as a gatekeeper to the scarce supply of decent, low rent housing, and understandably resented by some of those who could not obtain it. The experiences of poverty, racial discrimination and deprivation inevitably led to deep feelings of hostility to any "official agencies", and this was how at least some people now saw the Trust.

Suspicion was particularly strong amongst some members of the black community, who, not unreasonably, saw the Trust as yet another white-dominated organisation. This distrust led to threats against staff in the Trust's offices, disruption at public meetings and graffiti being posted with the words *"Don't trust the Trust"*.

On one occasion a young man, who was known to have a history of mental illness, produced a shotgun in the All Saints Road offices. Fortunately, those staff present were able to resolve the confrontation peacefully, but it raised the question of whether it was safe to continue having an open counter. The front-line staff, however, strongly opposed the suggestion of erecting a protective screen, on the grounds it would cut them off from the people of the area. The idea was dropped.

During the early 1970s there was an upsurge in squatting activity across London. The Trust was vulnerable to squatters, because it owned houses which were vacant whilst waiting for building work to start. People looking for somewhere to squat often felt it was safer to move in to a housing association property. Some private owners used force to recover possession of the property. Squatters expected that the Trust might allow them to stay until the properties they occupied were needed for building work to start, and would only evict them with a court order.

The Trust had a clear policy of taking action to evict squatters, so that the properties could be used to re-house the people in greatest need, as determined by their lettings policies. However, most of these were families with children or older people. Very few single people got re-housed, except when they were already tenants in properties which the Trust bought. Believing that they were discriminated against by the Trust, some single people squatted in empty properties and insisted that they were entitled to stay in them.

One dramatic confrontation came early one morning when a group calling themselves the Gay Commune, who were occupying 42 Colville Terrace, found themselves faced by the Trust's property buyer, Adrian Maynard, telling them they must be out by 11am that morning, or he would use *"reasonable force"* to make them leave. At 10am a group from the house went to the Trust's offices to try and negotiate an agreement. Peter Naish, the Area Manager, repeated over and over again that the Trust's policy was to evict squatters. It would not consider any group applying for a licence to occupy short-life property while such a group was occupying Trust property.

The members of the Commune argued that their eligibility for housing by the Trust should be considered, not as single men squatting but as a "family" in need of housing. It was their claim that they were not eligible for re-housing by either the Council or charitable housing trusts, which insisted on treating them as a collection of single men.

Negotiations had gone on during the week and John Coward went for tea with the Gay Commune on Friday. A few days later the Commune wrote a letter to the Committee of the Trust:

"We are one unmarried couple and a family of 12 gay men who decided to live together in a rented house in Brixton. There we were harassed by gangs of local queer-bashers to the degree of getting hit over the head with bottles, our front door smashed down, and having bricks thrown through all our windows. We were refused protection by the police, and within 24 hours we were given notice to quit. We came to Notting Hill principally because most of us had been squeezed out of rooms in the district in the first place.

We as gay men are as persecuted as any minority group (if not more). The difference between us and other minority groups is that we receive no help from any liberal institutions. We never qualify: where must we go? Back into our cells in lonely bedsits? We are continuously being told that we should integrate into the community. How can we when we are denied the privileges of the rest of the community? How can we when we cannot get anywhere to live?"

The outcome of the standoff was that John Coward told the group that the Trust would not offer them permanent re-housing, but it would be willing to make available a large short-life property where it would be possible for them to live together. It was deemed an honourable compromise by both sides.

In a later incident, a family which was squatting with two young children in one of the Trust's houses, arrived in the offices, accompanied by three young men. After a housing officer had explained why they did not have the priority needed to qualify immediately for permanent re-housing, they demanded to see John Coward. After John arrived to hear the demand repeated, the group threw him across the room when he tried to leave. He was knocked unconscious when his head hit the wall.

The setting up of the United Housing Association Trust
One different type of initiative for the Trust came from the creation of the United Housing Association Trust (UHAT) in 1970. It was set up with seven members/shareholders. These included the Notting Hill Housing Trust, Paddington Churches Housing Association, Family Housing Association, London and Quadrant Housing Trust and Second Actel Housing Association. John Coward was elected the Chairman.

With the exception of Second Actel, they were members of the new generation of associations, who saw UHAT as a means to complement their re-habilitation programmes by acquiring large new-build sites. The initiative clearly shows the ambitious goals of those associations.

The first project for UHAT came from the Greater London Council. With the Council elections due to take place in May 1973 the Conservative leadership of the GLC was looking for an initiative to mark its different approach to public housing from the Labour Party.

The proposal they made was that the Council would sell the Beaver Estate in Hounslow to UHAT. The estate, comprising 630 dwellings, had been planned as a normal council-owned estate. By selling to UHAT the GLC Conservatives wanted to demonstrate their policy of withdrawing from direct council ownership and management and of transferring this to a housing association. Though few predicted it at the time, this would eventually prove a major trend in housing management.

Under pressure to complete the sale before the Council elections took place, frantic late night negotiations were held to finalise the agreement and complete all the legal formalities. The sale was completed with the deadline imminent. As the Conservatives had feared, their party lost the election and the Labour Party re-took control of the GLC, lost four years earlier.

For UHAT the immediate advantage was that it would gain an instant presence and financial solidity which would be of advantage for negotiating further purchases. When it entered into the transaction the total resources of UHAT were £7 in its bank account from the £1 paid by the seven members for their membership shares. The purchase of the estate would also give UHAT a visible presence, and ownership would provide both income and an asset base which would be valuable in negotiating future acquisitions.

The risk was that if the Labour Party gained control of the GLC, it might blame UHAT for going ahead with the purchase so close to an election, and this might be damaging to UHAT's future prospects. In retrospect it seems surprising that the members of UHAT decided to take this risk, especially as many Labour Party members, including local councillors, were suspicious of housing associations in that era. Offending the newly elected Labour members on the GLC could have had far-reaching repercussions. Fortunately, the new Labour leadership was sympathetic to housing associations and retaining control of all the existing GLC stock was not one of its priorities.

The manager put in by UHAT to take charge of the Beaver estate was Alan Fell, who had come to the Trust as a volunteer shortly before, after leaving the family business in Birmingham where he had worked for the previous twenty years. Alan had no previous knowledge of housing management, but he was an experienced manager.

When UHAT took over, the estate was still under development, with some homes just occupied by new tenants, some completed but not yet let, and others just occupied by the first tenants. Alan Fell worked from an office based in one of the flats on the estate, which made access easy for tenants. GLC officers from the District Housing office were very helpful. The overall arrangements for the transfer to UHAT, the letting of the new tenancies and managing the estate went more smoothly than might have been anticipated. The gamble was a success.

The scale of housing need
Although the Trust was doing everything in its power to buy more properties, what it could do was still tiny in relation to the scale of the problem. Many of those in the worst housing need were large families, often living in two rooms or even a single room. Yet the Trust was given subsidies for each flat it produced, so it got more subsidy where a property was converted into several small flats rather than into larger flats or keeping it as a single family house. In addition, whilst the Trust could re-house more people where it bought an empty property, it was cheaper to buy properties with sitting tenants, who would need re-housing.

After the first few years the Trust found it had to keep closing its waiting list, until more properties were converted, because it had grown so long, and there was no prospect of re-housing the applicants for a long time into the future.

In 1971 Jeremy Sandford's book "Down and Out in Britain" was published. It was based on his research into the plight of homeless families several years after he had written the script for "Cathy Come Home".

He quotes the "Manager of the Notting Hill Housing Trust", who said:

"Every week ten or twelve desperate families come begging for accommodation and we are in the awful position of having to turn them away. I have the feeling that things are getting worse and worse with the continual reduction in rented accommodation. We have had to close our list to the larger families, who are the ones with the greatest need."

From the start the Trust had tried to keep rents as low as possible, so that they were affordable by tenants on low wages. However, it had still found that some tenants were not able to pay the rents and had set up a system of rent rebates to help them.

By 1972 the cost of these rebates to the Trust had risen to over £20,000, an increase of over £6,000 than the previous year. Fortunately, the 1972 Housing Finance Act required local authorities to set up a statutory Rent Rebate scheme, and many of the Trust's tenants became eligible for a "rent allowance", as it was called for private and housing association tenants.

The work of volunteers

The difficulties in securing adequate statutory funding in the early years made it necessary to do everything possible to minimize the cost of renovating properties bought by the Trust. One important way in which this was done was through the use of volunteers.

Martin Fenning worked with the central London branch of International Voluntary Service (IVS). His own family had experienced Rachmanism and he was personally very committed to tackling the housing problems in the area. He had stayed with Bruce Kenrick in the early days of the Trust, helping with decorating jobs, and when he was appointed the voluntary Project officer at IVS London he was keen to bring volunteers to help. Over the next few years IVS worked increasingly with the Trust, bringing volunteers in work parties to help. IVS saw such work as an ideal arrangement, since there were plenty of opportunities for useful jobs, which were well managed and supervised.

One of the most committed volunteers was Margaret McGavin (later Michael). She first came to help when she was the voluntary press officer for the IVS Central London. One of her duties was to agree press releases with John Coward for the local newspapers on the weekend workcamps.

She later became the Secretary of the Branch and took part regularly in volunteer workcamps over the next six years. There was one property at 245 Westbourne Park Road where volunteers worked over weekends for many months. As a result it was possible to convert the property into flats for two large families. Without the work of volunteers the Trust would have only been able to afford converting it into smaller flats. She remembers clearly the excitement of coming as a volunteer to Notting Hill and how motivated those who came were by *"the fibre"* of the Trust.

In 1970 Martin Fenning was appointed the Trust's first Volunteer Organiser. He worked from an office in the basement of 30 All Saints Road and the rest of the house was used as accommodation for up to 12 long term volunteers. Most weekends there were almost 30 volunteers, but on one celebrated Wednesday there were 73. During the summer IVS also ran International Workshops for volunteers from overseas who came and worked for 3 to 4 weeks. By this time the decorating was mostly done by the Building Section, but volunteers still carried out tasks such as clearing newly acquired properties, stripping paint and plaster, transporting furniture and helping tenants to move.

Volunteers also helped by visiting elderly tenants and others who needed help. On one occasion a pack of brownies planted daffodils in Colville Square, where the gardens had been opened for the use of tenants. On another occasion, large numbers of volunteers joined the Trust float "The Old Woman who lived in a Shoe" at the Notting Hill Carnival.

John Coward believes that the involvement of volunteers on such a significant scale was very important in influencing the ethos of the Trust. When he came, it was a new experience for him, as a seasoned local government officer, to have his letters typed by a very respectable local resident and to have a volunteer going round collecting the rents.

The volunteers came from a wide range of backgrounds, and included students, young professionals, middle-aged mothers and fiery left wing activists from overseas on IVS workcamps. They helped the Trust to extend its relationships within the local community and avoid becoming a closed bureaucracy.

Fundraising
The Trust's fundraising activity has been an immensely valuable part of its work from the very early days. Chapter 4 includes a summary of the money raised directly by the Trust, as well as the grants from Shelter, during the first ten years.

For the first few years the money raised by the Trust was vital in enabling houses to be bought, as the loans did not cover the full costs of purchase and rehabilitation. When it became possible to obtain 100% loans, more money was used to help tenants who could not afford to pay their rent, until a statutory rent rebate scheme was established.

When Pat White was appointed she took on responsibility for the Trust's fundraising and publicity, including producing new appeal literature and brochures for prospective individual donors.

In 1972 the Trust's opened its first charity shop in Putney and their number has grown steadily so that the Trust now runs a total of 30 shops over a wide area of London, in neighbourhoods both wealthy and modest. Initially the shops sold only second-hand goods, mostly clothing, but widened their activities to also sell new products. They have not only been an important source of income but have also provided good public relations, as people see the Trust's name prominently shown above every shop front.

For several years the Trust organised a fundraising event in the Town Hall in Kensington High Street, with stalls selling donated goods. Frankie Morgan (later Merz) was a volunteer supporter who organised it, and subsequently was a committee member for many years. She recalls:

"We had the world's poshest fair every year for housing the people in North Kensington. I still find it absolutely extraordinary, the great and the good of Kensington and Chelsea used to turn up for this fair and spend a lot of money. If you had asked any of them what it was for I don't know if anybody would have known".

Through a friend, who worked for the Duchess of Gloucester, Frankie was able to interest the Duchess in the work of the Trust, and she accepted an invitation to become its Patron. Over the years she has opened new developments and attended a number of events, all of which have provided very good publicity for the Trust.

One high profile initiative was the full-page Loan Notes Prospectus in the Financial Times, inviting readers to lend money at nil interest, as well as give donations. The £22,500 given in loans was disappointing, but the feature also led to a donation of £10,000 from a man who had grown up in the neighbourhood where the Trust worked, and the novelty of the prospectus yielded favourable editorial publicity.

The Trust's finances

The following table sets out an analysis of the sources of the Trust's finances, and the uses to which they were put, over its first fourteen years. The only positive contributor to accumulated revenue surplus was the remainder of each year's fundraising income after funding support for tenants. This was the vital stream of income that the Trust used to finance the purchase and renovation of properties before, if ever, mortgage finance was obtained. In the 1970s it also provided financing for the mounting revenue deficits that, from 1974 onwards, were eligible, after lengthy delays, for funding by Revenue Deficit Grant.

The support given to tenants that was paid out of fundraising income was adminstered by the Trust's welfare staff and also included rent rebates to tenants unable to pay the rent without financial assistance. Only after the 1972 Housing Act was there a national scheme of rent allowances for low income tenants.

Notting Hill Housing Trust

Sources of Finance 1964-1977

	Sources of Finance				*Total*	*Financing*	
Period to	Accum. Revenue Surplus	Loan Stock, Loan Notes	Mortgages	Bank Overdraft/ (balance)		Housing Properties (less HAG from 1976)	Other Net (Liabilities) /Assets
	£k	£k	£k	£k	£k	£k	£k
	(Note 1)	(Note 2)	(Note 3)	(Note 4)			
12/64	37	10	0	(22)	25	32	(7)
12/65	78	23	25	(22)	104	113	(9)
12/66	123	30	162	2	317	312	5
12/67	188	33	371	100	692	701	(9)
9/68	242	31	672	76	1,021	1,030	(9)
9/69	308	34	1,170	69	1,587	1,615	(34)
9/70	378	34	1,999	68	2,479	2,517	(38)
9/71	415	31	3,037	77	3,560	3,700	(140)
9/72	384	42	4,262	202	4,890	5,020	(130)
9/73	345	61	6,841	314	7,561	7,733	(172)
9/74	235	75	10,601	406	11,317	11,557	(240)
9/75	265	72	15,331	601	16,269	16,440	(171)
9/76	150	87	23,658	232	24,127	24,803	(676)
9/77	(81)	78	31,460	441	31,898	33,072	(1,174)

Table Notes:
1. Throughout these years, income from rents was always insufficient to cover the costs of managing the tenancies and maintaining the housing properties. This "property revenue" deficit and the cost of welfare support for tenants, was financed from fundraising income. This column shows the accumulated amounts of the remaining fundraising income that were available to invest in properties up to 1971. Then, as deficits mounted, (and, from 1973-4, when Revenue Deficit Grant was treated as income only when the Department of the Environment had eventually agreed its payment) the accumulation was also used, together with bank overdraft facilities, in "bridging" the deficits. By 1977 the Trust had no positive reserves, other than that received as Housing Association Grant.
2. Loan stock and loan notes were low, or "nil", interest loans from Trust supporters, repayable on three months' notice.
3. Mortgage loans were first obtained in 1965 from a building society. Subsequently they were sourced from the GLC and local authorities. In the mid-1970's the Housing Corporation became the principal source.
4. The bank overdraft was secured on the value of some unmortgaged properties.

Chapter 4

LAUNCHING SHELTER

In the two years after the Trust was launched, Bruce Kenrick continued to make an extraordinary number of radio and television appearances, especially remarkable since the Trust was only a small, local organisation.

Donations in 1965 raised £81,000, including proceeds from a second national advertising campaign. However, the costs of the advertising were £34,000 and some members of the Committee were becoming concerned at the amount being spent on advertising, and were also worried that the Trust was growing too fast. These disagreements led to lengthy arguments in the Committee meetings and friction between some members and Bruce, who was Chair. On several occasions minutes of the previous meeting were challenged, and had to be re-written before being approved.

Bruce Kenrick was disappointed by what he regarded as slow progress in buying properties and providing new housing. He had been the leading advocate of national advertising campaigns, but was becoming convinced that a purely local housing association could not raise as much money as a national organisation.

He had also been helping to start housing associations in several other cities, and saw this as a key part of the Trust's role. The committee minutes refer to two of the new associations as "Daughter Trusts", although it is doubtful if they saw themselves as such!

The first of these was in Liverpool, where the full-time staff member of the Student Christian Movement (SCM) at Liverpool University had come to visit Notting Hill. On his return home he brought together a group to set up the Liverpool Housing Trust.

This new association was formally registered on 14 March 1965, the day before the SCM held a housing conference in Liverpool to raise awareness amongst students about the crisis of bad housing in inner city areas. It was chaired by Bruce Kenrick, the final speech of the conference was given by Rev. Richard Holloway, then an Anglican priest working in the Gorbals area of Glasgow, who was to become the Bishop of Edinburgh. He made a passionate call for action to tackle the injustice of squalid housing in Britain's inner cities.

Two SCM members at the conference, Liz Clutton and Kit Norton, went back to Birmingham convinced of the need for a new housing association to tackle the housing problems there. They invited Bruce Kenrick to come and meet two friends: David Mumford, a City councillor who would later become the first Director of the new Birmingham Housing Trust (BHT) and the Rev. John Duncan, an Anglican priest. They were to serve as Chair and Chief Executive of the new trust, and of the Copec Housing Association with which BHT merged in 1970, for over twenty five years.

However, some disquiet was caused by Bruce Kenrick's activities in promoting new associations. The Trust's Committee minutes record a letter from Rev. George McLeod, a sponsor of the Trust, who was the founder of the Iona Community and a leading member of the Church of Scotland. His letter voiced concerns that had been conveyed to him from people in Glasgow, Birmingham and Liverpool, that the Notting Hill Housing Trust was seeking to set up new housing associations in those areas without proper consultation with local people, especially with associations which already existed.

A new housing association formed close to Notting Hill was the Paddington Churches Housing Association, now the largest member of the Genesis Housing Group. As so often, the churches were involved. The idea for setting up the Association came from Rev. Ken Bartlett, a young curate at the Anglican Church in Sussex Gardens in Paddington. Most members of the church were affluent, middle-aged people, but some of the children coming to the Sunday School were living in overcrowded and insecure flats. Having tried unsuccessfully for several months to find unfurnished flats at affordable rents for some of those families, he decided there must be a better solution.

Another member of the Paddington Christian Council, which Ken Bartlett had helped to form, was Rev. Robin Sharp, the minister at the Methodist church in Fernhead Road in north Paddington. He had recently come from the staff of the Student Christian Movement, was shocked by the housing conditions in the area and frustrated by the inward-looking attitudes of most of the church community.

Together they got a grant of £900 from a charitable trust, recruited members to form a committee – including the Mayor of Paddington Council, and set up the new Association. Ken Bartlett was appointed the Secretary. One of his first actions was to ask Bruce Kenrick for advice, who suggested he speak to John Coward. So began one of the most influential partnerships in the expansion of the housing association movement over the next decade.

For the first three years Paddington Churches had no full-time staff. In 1967 a grant of £9,000 from Shelter enabled the association to appoint a full-time Director. However, after the interviewing committee decided not to appoint any of the candidates, John Coward suggested to Ken Bartlett that he should do it himself. When his bishop gave the same advice – at least until a suitable post in an ecumenical inner city church arose – Ken Bartlett decided to apply and was appointed. He went on to become its first Director, and became the Chair of Shelter during the early 1970s.

The New Islington and Hackney Housing Association is another organisation formed in the early 1960s by a group of individuals very similar to those who set up the Notting Hill and Paddington Churches associations. Their first meeting was called in late 1964 by the local Divisional School Care Organiser, Kathleen Chew.

They decided to ask for help from volunteers in raising money, and shortly afterwards were put in touch with *"two bright young men from the Catholic Church"*. These were Simon MacLachlan and Charles Wood, who were to become Chair and Treasurer of the Association for many years. Another early committee member was Peter Dixon, who was a member of the committee for over twenty years, including serving as the Treasurer and Chair. In 2003 he was appointed the Chair of the Housing Corporation.

Like the others in inner London, the association concentrated on buying and renovating street properties. Their 25th anniversary publication chronicles their progress through different phases: *"the volunteer days, the age of the gifted amateur, the period of rapid growth, the era of professionalism and the social housing business"*. It is a description which could have been aptly applied to a number of the other housing associations formed in the 1960s in inner city areas.

The launch of Shelter

The experiences of helping to set-up and promote new associations made Bruce Kenrick more convinced than ever of the need for a national organisation, separate from the Trust. His initial plan was for the Notting Hill Housing Trust to expand to become a national organisation, but other members of the Committee believed the Trust should remain a local organisation. However, the Committee did agree to support Bruce in setting up a new national body, and after much discussion he succeeded in gaining the backing of four national organisations, the Housing Association Charitable Trust, which was the fundraising arm of the National Federation of Housing Societies; the Catholic Housing Aid Society; Christian Action, the sponsor of the Housing the Homeless Fund; and the British Churches

Housing Trust. All of them agreed to suspend any national fundraising appeals in order to support Shelter's.

In the autumn of 1966 plans were developed for the launch of the new organisation, to be called Shelter. It was decided to offer the money raised by its national appeal to eight housing associations. As well as Notting Hill, these included the new associations which the Trust had supported, Paddington Churches Housing Association, Birmingham Housing Trust and Liverpool Housing Trust. The other four associations were the Kensington Housing Trust, Copec in Birmingham, Liverpool Improved Housing, and Mulberry Housing Trust in Paddington.

The inclusion of the already established associations was an important gesture in recognising that the new associations were not seeking to replace already established ones. The Birmingham Housing Trust and Copec merged in 1970, and more recently became the Prime Focus Housing Group. Liverpool Improved Housing, an existing association formed in 1928, welcomed the offer of Shelter funding and continued to receive Shelter support over the next few years. It has since expanded to become the Riverside Housing Group, one of the largest associations in the country.

However, both the Mulberry and Kensington Trusts turned down the offer of grants. The Chair of Mulberry was Sir Keith Joseph, who had been the Minister of Housing in the previous Conservative Government and would later provide some of the intellectual foundations of Thatcherism. He wanted to show that housing associations could succeed without relying on public subsidy or charitable donation. As his critics predicted, however, he was unsuccessful in his aim and Mulberry was taken over by the St Marylebone Housing Association, now absorbed into Octavia Housing and Care.

In deciding to back the launch of Shelter, the Committee of the Notting Hill Housing Trust agreed not to continue with appeals outside the Royal Borough of Kensington and Chelsea in return for an assurance that Shelter would pass on to it similar amounts of money to those which the Trust had been raising in previous years from its own appeals. There were lengthy discussions in the Trust committee on whether its mailing list of donors could be used in an appeal for Shelter. The agreement finally reached was the donor list should be used, but that the labels for the mailing had to be typed in the Trust's offices so that Shelter couldn't re-use them in the future without the Trust's agreement.

During the year before the launch of Shelter Bruce Kenrick's energy was directed almost wholly towards that goal. What turned out to be a crucial decision was the appointment of a go-getting New Zealander, Des Wilson, as the research officer. The research Des carried out in visiting families living in desperately overcrowded conditions in Notting Hill convinced him that what was needed was a new kind of campaigning organisation. It should be one which saw its role not as a conventional charity but as one fired by anger at the injustice which trapped people in such appalling conditions.

There were two other people whose support for setting up Shelter was very important. Lewis Waddilove, the Chair of the National Federation of Housing Societies, was the immensely respected Director of the Joseph Rowntree Foundation and had served as a member of the Milner Holland Committee. Father Eammon Casey was the dynamic Director of the Catholic Housing Aid Society, who became the first Director of the Shelter Housing Aid Centre (SHAC) before returning to Ireland to become the Bishop of Kerry.

Shelter was launched on 1st December 1966. It came ten days after the showing of the TV drama documentary "Cathy Come Home", written by Jeremy Sandford and directed by Ken Loach, then not as well-known as he would later become. Based on research into the conditions which homeless families experienced in temporary accommodation and the desperate shortage of accommodation in Britain's inner cities, the film showed with dramatic power how a family, Cathy's, could be broken up by the brutal realities of homelessness.

"Cathy Come Home" has been voted the most influential television documentary in British social history. The title itself became a tabloid synonym for homeless people and it is firmly associated in many minds with the launch of Shelter. In fact the timing of the two events was an extraordinary coincidence. In the less media-sophisticated Sixties the founders of Shelter had no advance knowledge of the showing of "Cathy Come Home". Des Wilson has said that he had been unaware of the first showing.

"Cathy Come Home" had an enormous impact on the country. What shocked decent people in all walks of life was not just the dramatic portrayal of how a young family could end up homeless, but also the brutal treatment such families could receive at the hands of both agents of private landlords and public officials. Many viewers believed that the post-war welfare state had put an end to such callousness, and were deeply shocked by the programme. Especially unsettling were the final shots of two young children being forcibly separated from their mother and taken into care, simply because the family did not have a home.

When Shelter was launched ten days later at St Martins-in-the-Fields Church in central London it received huge publicity. As well as numerous news reports, Shelter itself had placed a full double-spread two page appeal in the Times newspaper. The first page contained articles by Des Wilson, Lewis Waddilove and Bruce Kenrick, and the second an appeal for money, with a photograph of a mother and child above the caption "Home Sweet Hell".

Shelter's fundraising appeals powerfully showed what it described as a national housing crisis, and asked for donations to the housing associations it had agreed to support.

Prior to the launch Des Wilson's formal role had been as researcher, the position to which Bruce had appointed him. Following the huge impact made by the launch the Trustees believed it was essential to appoint a Director, and wanted to appoint Des to this position. But Bruce Kenrick vigorously opposed this, believing Wilson to be unsuitable. When he was unable to persuade the other Trustees during a difficult and acrimonious discussion, Bruce resigned both as Chair of Shelter and as a Trustee. He has since played no role in Shelter.

One persistent cause of regret within the Trust was the failure of Shelter in the years following its launch to recognise the role that Bruce Kenrick and the Trust played in its inception. In his book "They Said It Was The Place's Fault", Des Wilson responded to the question he was often asked: "Who was responsible for setting up Shelter?". He wrote *no one person was responsible for Shelter*" and makes no reference at all to Bruce's unique role in conceiving the idea of a national housing campaign, gaining the support of existing national organisations, and leading the huge amount of work in planning Shelter's launch.

However, Eammon Casey, who succeeded Bruce as the Chair of Shelter, has no doubts about his role. In an interview for this book he said: *"It was Bruce Kenrick who started Shelter and without him it would never have existed"*.

Shelter's grants to the Trust

Over the seven years from 1967 Shelter made grants of £262,000 to the Notting Hill Housing Trust. This ended in 1974 when the new Housing Act provided statutory funding for the development activity of associations.

The annual grants from Shelter to the Trust were lower than the amounts which had been raised by the Trust in each of its first three years. The total income from donations, however, was considerably higher because many supporters of the Trust's earlier appeals continued to give money.

The Trust's Fund-raising from 1964 to 1974

Date	Donations (£)	Costs (£)	Net (£)	Shelter (£)	Total (£)
1964	58,126	20,000	38,126	-	38,126
1965	81,499	34,165	47,334	-	47,334
1966	62,262	4,889	57,773	-	57,773
1967	37,377	2,033	35,344	40,000	75,344
1968*	23,811	360	23,451	32,500	55,951
1969	45,783	2,566	43,217	43,000	86,217
1970	35,930	5,941	29,989	57,500	87,489
1971	59,861	7,703	52,158	33,230	85,388
1972	39,046	10,104	28,942	38,255	67,197
1973	70,216	16,160	54,056	14,008	68,064
1974	71,327	21,831	49,496	3,437	52,933

The table above shows donations to the Trust from 1963 to 1974, including both money raised directly and the Shelter donations. In the three years prior to Shelter's launch, the Trust raised an annual of average of £48,000. In the six years that followed the combined income from Shelter and the Trust's own fundraising averaged £76,000. Despite ending its own direct advertising appeals, total donations to the Trust were on average £28,000 a year higher after Shelter was set up than before.

The value of the Shelter grants to the Trust may be better appreciated if they are translated into today's prices.

Year to December 1967	£40k	becomes	£416,000
9 months to September 1968	£33k	"	£320,000
Year to September 1969	£43k	"	£406,000
Year to September 1970	£58k	"	£508,000
Year to September 1971	£33k	"	£260,000
Year to September 1972	£38k	"	£277,000
Year to September 1973	£14k	"	£93,000
Year to September 1974	£3k	"	£16,000

* The figure for 1968 relates only to a 9 month period to 30 September 1968. This therefore excludes the month of October in which the Trust sent out its major annual appeal to its mailing list which explains the reduced level of donations in that year.

(The current value of the donations is calculated by using the retail price index of 182.6 at October 2003, where January 1987 = 100).

The Trust itself raised £58,126 in the twelve months to December 1964, which after deducting advertising costs of £19,999 gave a net income of £38,127. Using the same formula as above gives a net fundraising income of £445,344 at today's prices.

Chapter 5

A CAULDRON OF
COMMUNITY ACTIVITY

For a decade from the mid 1960s, Notting Hill was a cauldron of community activity. A whole range of new organisations were formed, and an intensive campaign was waged to change the housing policies of the Borough Council.

Initially the Notting Hill Housing Trust, which was still a small organisation, did not play a leading role in the campaign. As the pressure on the Council grew, however, the Trust emerged as a key agency in the development of new policies.

Kensington and Chelsea Council was Conservative-controlled, as had been both the constituent authorities before the new Council was formed through amalgamation in 1965. The overwhelming majority of the councillors represented the mainly prosperous residents in the central and southern parts of the borough, which also contained the smart shops of Kensington High Street – where Biba was at the height of its fame – Knightsbridge and Chelsea, as well as a range of famous museums, university institutions and musical centres.

The housing problems in the Borough were very heavily concentrated in North Kensington, well to the north of tree-lined Holland Park Avenue and largely out of sight of affluent residents. The local authority had built fewer council homes than any other in inner London, and had carried out fewer major slum clearance and redevelopment schemes in the post-war years. The Milner Holland report had documented the high concentration of very poor housing conditions in North Kensington, and called for urgent action by the local authorities.

There had been very little response by the Royal Borough, and it had been strongly criticised for its complacency. The main policy used for improving the poor conditions in privately rented housing was a programme of public health inspections, with notices served on landlords whose properties failed to comply with the required standards. However, progress in serving notices had been very slow and the rate of compliance disappointing.

In the majority of London boroughs almost all new socially rented homes since the war had been built by the local authorities, and the role of housing associations had been negligible. In wealthy Kensington and Chelsea, however, there were a number of charitable housing associations, some of which had been active in North Kensington since the early part of the century.

The Octavia Hill and Rowe Trusts had built small family homes in the Notting Dale area, and had a reputation as sympathetic and friendly landlords, but because of the lack of public subsidy they had not carried out any new developments since World War II.

In the inter-war period two large estates had been built in the north-west of the borough by the Peabody Trust and the Sutton Dwellings Trust. Their policy was to give priority in lettings when any flats became vacant to the sons and daughters of existing tenants. The policy may not have been deliberately discriminatory against black newcomers, but that was undoubtedly the effect.

The most active of the housing associations was the Kensington Housing Trust (KHT) set up in the 1920s by socially minded residents from the southern part of the borough. Its Chair, and later President, was Lord Burleigh, for many years also a senior Conservative councillor, and several of the active members of KHT also served at different times as councillors. KHT was seen by the Borough Council as the best way of providing good quality rented homes in the north of the Borough, given its reluctance to build new Council estates itself.

Although no public criticisms were made, the Kensington Housing Trust was critical of the Notting Hill Housing Trust, especially of its high public profile. This view was also shared by the other older housing trusts in the area, who disapproved of the "brash new kid on the block", which they feared was damaging their hard-won respectability.

Four years earlier KHT had decided to expand its work in order to house tenants who were threatened with homelessness as the result of the controversial 1957 Rent Act. It started a programme of buying houses that were for sale in order to house families threatened with eviction. The Borough Council had agreed to provide loans for purchasing and renovating these properties.

KHT's Annual Reports give several graphic examples of how this was done. One example was the purchase of eight houses in Lancaster Road, North Kensington, which were offered for sale:

"Twelve of the lettings were decontrolled, which meant that the tenants would be evicted from them when the sale to a speculative buyer took place in order to buy empty properties which could be let at a high rent. Several tenants had been

given notice to quit and one had already applied to the Trust as a prospective homeless family.... Since the main work of the Trust at the moment is to provide for, or to prevent, the creation of homelessness it was decided that the property must be bought".

KHT's Annual Report for 1964 records that:

"Over the previous five years the Trust has housed 115 families, a total of 439 people, and has prevented 76 other families from becoming homeless, by buying the houses from which they were about to be evicted. For this purpose it has purchased 107 houses containing 329 tenancies".

Looking back it is striking to see how strong the similarities were between what the Kensington Housing Trust was doing and the activities of the Notting Hill Housing Trust a few years later. However, KHT rarely sought publicity for its activities, and little was known about it. In contrast, Bruce Kenrick obtained a high profile for the Notting Hill Housing Trust from its very first days and the Trust secured a lot of publicity for its work in buying properties to prevent tenants being evicted and to house families who had lost their homes.

In its major report on "Housing in London" the Milner Holland Committee, examined in some detail the contribution of housing associations to meeting London's housing needs. Its report cited the Ministry of Housing and Local Government's returns showing that housing associations had contributed 4,422 dwellings in London since 1945. This compares with over 400,000 built by local authorities during that time.

The old charitable trusts, such as Peabody and William Sutton, had been endowed initially with large philanthropic donations. In the absence of such funding they had carried out little development since the war. The older industrial societies had only been able to construct new dwellings where there was a surplus from pre-war flats which enabled them to cross-subsidize new properties. The view of the Committee was that:

"The scope for expansion by the larger charitable trusts is limited by their policies in raising capital for new development. If these associations are to play a significant role in the redevelopment of large areas of London..... then these policies must clearly be changed.

Since the Second World War.... the contribution of housing associations has been marginal. We value the work of charitable bodies at present raising funds to buy and convert properties and thus relieve the plight of some of London's homeless. Admirable though this work is, however, it will in our view continue to be marginal. It will continue to be in the nature of an emergency measure. It is not a pattern for a large scale contribution to London's housing by the housing association movement". [1]

This view of housing associations was widely accepted at the time, not least by many Labour politicians. Housing associations owned only 1% of the housing stock nationally. They had practically no national profile, and were almost unknown to many people. They were often seen as old-fashioned and, at worst, as moribund organisations. Very few associations had carried out any new development since 1945, with the exception of the associations developing sheltered housing for older people.

Most people who argued for a higher housing programme called for more homes to be built by local authorities. During the 1950s the Labour Party had adopted a policy for the municipalisation of all privately rented housing, with direct management by local authorities, who would be responsible either for bringing them up to adequate standards or replacing them with new homes. Yet this policy had been dropped, even before the 1964 General Election, as too complex and ambitious.

New community organisations in Notting Hill
In the autumn of 1966, the arrival in the area of the Notting Hill Community Workshop was a significant landmark in the development of community initiatives.

The plans for setting up the Workshop had come from George Clark, a seasoned veteran of the Campaign for Nuclear Disarmament (CND) and the more militant anti-nuclear Committee of 100. His ideas drew on experience from the politics of the New Left and the peace movement, and also from Students for Democratic Society (SDS) and new community movements in the United States. Clark had a reputation of being difficult to work with, and following disagreements with other members, he resigned from the Workshop in 1968. Subsequently he worked with the Notting Hill Housing Service, which was formed to run an advice service.

The Community Workshop consisted of a core of members who committed themselves to living in the area and seeking to develop new forms of grassroots activity. Their belief was that change in deprived, inner city neighbourhoods should be achieved through the active participation of the people living in those areas. They argued that the style of activity of the political parties was irrelevant and that the existing power structures ignored the needs of low income residents in North Kensington. They were critical of the paternalism of traditional voluntary agencies and sought to work with local residents to develop a new style of community action.

The Community Workshop set up in a house at 60 St Ervans Road, just off the Golborne Road, and started to explore what it saw as the most burning problems in the area. The Workshop's full-time organiser was John

O'Malley. He was 27 when he came to Notting Hill, after several years teaching maths in a south London comprehensive school. He had thought carefully about new ways of achieving change in an area such as Notting Hill. Central to this was working with local residents and supporting community-led campaigns, but also developing alliances with individuals and agencies who could widen the base of support for community initiatives as well as help influence the political decision-making structures.

John and Jan O'Malley had married just before coming to Notting Hill. John O'Malley played a pivotal role in the complex network of relationships that developed between different agencies. For the next two years Jan was still a student at Oxford University, but became one of the leading community activists, especially after coming to live full-time in the area. She had grown up in Liverpool, where her father had been Bruce Kenrick's doctor, and who had diagnosed the faulty treatment he had received for his malaria.

The battle over Colville Gardens

The first public initiative of the Workshop came with the setting up of the Notting Hill People's Association. This followed a front page article in the Guardian in January 1967 which broke the news that one of the largest private landlords in North Kensington, the Bowen Davies company, was facing liquidation and the owner was planning to sell its properties. The portfolio included a group of substantial properties at 1–9 Colville Gardens, containing a warren of bed-sits let as furnished tenancies.

Fearful of being evicted, several tenants decided that collective action was needed, and were given support by members of the Community Workshop. 400 people attended a packed meeting in the hall of the All Saints Church, immediately opposite the Colville Gardens houses. A few days later the Notting Hill People's Association was formed, with tenants from Colville Gardens and members of the Workshop taking on committee roles.

After strong lobbying of local councillors, an emergency resolution was passed by the Council instructing the Housing Committee to prepare a detailed report on the properties owned by the Bowen Davies Group of Companies. However, when the report was produced it was seen as a whitewash, ignoring many of the defects in the properties and describing their condition as *"better than average for the area"*. It was a description that evoked fury amongst members of the People's Association.

In response, the Association drew up a detailed analysis, which documented the severe overcrowding and extensive defects in the properties. For example, two flats consisting of a double bedsitting room, with shared toilet and bathroom, were each occupied by seven adults and four children.

Long lists of disrepair were documented. There were numerous complaints about mismanagement. The report showed that the nine properties were occupied by 202 people in 70 different tenancies. Over a third of those living in the properties were children under 10.

When the report was submitted to the Council in April 1967 members of the People's Association attended the meeting and were outraged when the councillors accepted the formal report to the Housing Committee and ignored their response. They protested loudly from the public gallery, and one member was so outraged that he jumped on the table around which the councillors were sitting, crying *"There is only one question about these councillors: Are they fools or are they knaves?"* The response from the Mayor was to order the gallery to be cleared.

Over the next two years the campaign over the future of the properties at 1-9 Colville Gardens developed into an epic struggle, initially to try and prevent Bowen Davies evicting the existing tenants so they could sell the properties with vacant possession, and then to persuade the local authority to ensure that they passed into the hands of a reputable social landlord.

The properties had been bought for £8,000 by Davies Investment in 1954. In 1968 the Kensington Housing Trust offered to buy them for £47,000 – allegedly with the support of the Council - which was the maximum amount the district valuer would approve. This offer was refused and the property was instead sold to a Bahamas-based company. A year later they were re-sold to another property developer, who immediately began evicting the tenants and turning the houses into luxury flats. The only concession wrested from the new owner was to make a payment to the Notting Hill Housing Trust in return for it re-housing twelve of the tenants.

Phyliss Danny, an Afro-Caribbean woman, and her four children were one of those families re-housed by the Trust from their overcrowded flat at 8 Colville Gardens. Initially she moved to a flat in Westbourne Park Road, but since 1978 has lived in a four bedroom flat in St Luke's Road. She is very happy with her flat and especially the space it has given to bring up her children.

In Colville Gardens the whole family had been living in just one room, sharing a bathroom and toilet with other tenants in the house. For four years she lived with the fear of being evicted with nowhere else to go. She joined the People's Association when it was formed and was active in the campaign to get the houses bought by a housing association:

"I was given a lot of support, especially by Pat McDonald (a tenant who was the Secretary of the People's Association), John O'Malley and Peter Kandler (a solicitor who was a member of the Community Workshop) and other members of the

Association. Another person who helped me was Father Peter Clarke, the priest at the All Saints Church opposite Colville Gardens. He baptised all my children. I've now been a member of that church for over forty years.

Everyone supported each other" she recalls. *"There were English people, Irish, West Indian and lots of other nationalities. The children played together in the street, and we all fought to have the garden opened so they could have somewhere safe to play".*

Her only regret is that all but one of her grown up children had to move away from the area to find somewhere to live, and are now living across London in Thamesmead, Stratford and Neasden. One daughter who is now a social worker in Brent still lives at home, as well as a teenage grandson. She is a registered foster carer, and has been taking children to look after for many years.

For years, many people living in Notting Hill had not only endured appalling physical conditions, but also a strong sense of powerlessness. They felt that the decisions about their homes and community were almost all taken by agencies from outside the area.

Private tenants found their landlords selling the properties where they lived without their knowledge. The first they knew was often when a new owner served them with notice to quit. The experience of the tenants in 1–9 Colville Gardens became a dramatic symbol of the unaccountable power of landlords.

The more radical community organisations strongly criticised the Council of the Royal Borough for its inactivity, with extensive media publicity and demonstrations. Squatters occupied empty properties to dramatize the scandal of decent properties standing empty cheek by jowl with such acute housing need.

The Notting Hill Carnival was started in 1965, mostly by a small group of West Indians and Rhaune Laslett, who ran an advice service from the front room of her own home in Tavistock Crescent.

After years of tension over the sometimes heavy-handed way it was policed, the Carnival, by now a tourist event, was increasingly run on the organisers' terms. There were still incidents, but the vast crowds were generally peaceful and exuberant. Newspaper photographs of police officers and revellers exchanging headgear or dancing together in the street became something of a media cliché. But what it symbolised to a once-marginalised community was that, if only for a few days a year, they "owned" Notting Hill.

Every week the People's Association held an open meeting in the All Saints Hall attended by members of local tenants groups, black organisations, advice centres and a range of community organisations. Each week it published the People's News, with reports of decisions by the Council, campaigning activities and events in the local community.

In August 1967 another high profile event was the Notting Hill Summer Project, which brought 100 volunteers to live and work in the area for four weeks. One of the volunteers was Ann Warden, who went on to become the Labour Parliamentary candidate for Kensington in three elections, failing to get elected by only 800 votes at the by-election in 1988. Others included Christopher Hitchens, now a controversial right-wing journalist in the United States, and Patrick Barlow, the well-known TV actor.

The Notting Hill Housing Survey

The Summer Project was initiated by the Community Workshop and organised through a broad coalition of community organisations. The main activity was a door-to-door housing survey which documented the housing conditions in the three areas with the worst housing problems, the Golborne, Lancaster Road and Colville areas. The Project also ran three Neighbourhood Housing Advice Centres and Play Schemes during the school holidays providing activities for children.

In addition several public meetings were held with prominent speakers including Peter Townsend, well known for his work on the growth of poverty in Britain, and Stuart Hall, a leading member of the New Left. A Panorama programme was produced which showed the social conditions in Notting Hill and filmed the activity of the volunteers.

The report of the Housing Survey was published in May 1969. The conditions were worse than those reported in the Milner Holland study, based on the 1961 Census five years earlier. The three neighbourhoods of North Kensington covered by the survey were those believed to be the worst in the whole area. Its findings were shocking:

- One third of all households were living at a density of more than one and a half people per room, and over two thirds of all children in the survey lived in flats with too few bedrooms.

- The worst conditions were experienced mostly by black tenants, paying high rents for insecure furnished rooms.

The recommendations of the Housing Service, which published the survey, focused mainly on the importance of increasing the number of rents that were registered and changes to rent legislation to strengthen the security of furnished tenants. It also stressed strongly the future role of the Housing Service itself in providing advice and support to tenants.

The report was launched by George Clark to a packed meeting of over 200 local residents in the Lancaster Road Methodist Church on 5 May 1969. However, Clark's speech was followed by the presentation of what was termed "a first response" by a group of community activists who called for a more critical attack on the Council's record and more radical policies for tackling the problems. Their statement argued that:

"The primary responsibility for the condition of housing in Notting Hill must rest with the Council of the Royal Borough of Kensington and Chelsea. They have built fewer houses, levy lower rates, give less housing subsidy and charge higher rents than any other comparable London borough".

It criticised the Council's housing inspection programme in the Colville and Tavistock areas, which had been launched as a "three year emergency programme" in 1963. In 1969 it was still not completed. 1,534 houses had been inspected, with action required to bring them up to standard in 1,261 of these. 2,583 statutory notices under the Housing or Public Health Acts had been served; 32,980 re-inspections had been carried out; but work had been completed satisfactorily on only 573 properties.

The "first response" shared the conclusion of the Housing Survey Report that the problems could only be solved through a massive programme, involving the Greater London Council and central Government, as well as the Borough Council. It also set out a range of specific measures which should be taken, including that:

"All property in disrepair through owner's neglect should be acquired by compulsory purchase.... Similarly property should be bought by compulsory purchase to prevent conversion to luxury developments... The Borough Council should refuse planning permission for improvements that would make accommodation unaffordable".

The mood of the meeting showed strong backing for the calls for urgent and radical action. There was publicity for the report of the Housing Survey, nationally as well as locally. As a result of the criticism of its housing record over the previous few years, Kensington and Chelsea Council was becoming notorious for its failure to tackle the conditions in North Kensington.

In April 1969 Princess Margaret came to open the Notting Hill Housing Trust's new flats and offices in All Saints Road. Outside a group of local people took the opportunity to protest about the Council's failure to tackle the housing problems in the area.

The community organisations were becoming more and more angry about the problems tenants were facing. In 1969 the People's Association started to produce a weekly paper. It was put together each Sunday evening by members of the Association and circulated around North Kensington. It covered a wide range of issues, including the availability of play facilities, provision for young people, benefit problems and relationships with the police. The issue that dominated was housing.

The range and frequency of the problems were shocking:

• Tenants being harassed by landlords, and some even illegally evicted from their homes.
• Landlords failing to carry out urgent repairs.
• Landlords charging exorbitant rents.
• Furnished tenants facing eviction because their landlords planned to sell with vacant possession.
• Furnished tenants in clearance areas deemed not entitled to re-housing when their homes were demolished.

In response community organisations were taking action to advise and support tenants who were facing difficulties.

The opening of the Law Centre in July 1970 marked an important advance in the help given to tenants. The People's News "Review of the Year for 1971" summarised some of the Centre's activities over its first 18 months. It had applied for 29 injunctions on behalf of tenants to stop illegal actions, and all but three had been granted by the Court. Two landlords and one troublesome "boyfriend" had been committed to prison for contempt of court. All but five of the cases related to landlord/tenant problems.

The Council begins to take action
The findings of the Housing Survey report caused concern in the Department of the Environment. In early June 1969 the Minister of Housing, Anthony Greenwood, called representatives of the Council to a meeting in his office. After conveying the Labour Government's concern at the acute housing problems in North Kensington, he asked the Council to draw up detailed and comprehensive plans for either redevelopment or rehabilitation.

This meeting galvanized the Council into action. The previous year, the Council had elected a new Leader, Sir Malby Crofton. He was a confident, old Etonian, in his mid-40s, a member of the London Stock Exchange, and with a hereditary baronetcy. He had only been a member of the Council since 1962.

The candidate who had been expected to win the election for Leader was Councillor Baldwin. He had been the Chair of the Finance Committee for the previous four years, and a member of the Council since 1952. As one committee chair put it: *"By all the usual signs Baldwin should have had it. He had length of service, whereas Crofton was a new boy. He* (Baldwin) *was well-known to all the councillors".*

The first vote had been a dead-heat, and Malby Crofton won the second ballot. He wanted the Council to take a less defensive, more proactive approach towards the problems in North Kensington. As he and his colleagues began to look for new policies, the attractions of what the housing associations could offer became greater.

The Council was adamant that it would not undertake a major programme of municipalisation in North Kensington, but the evidence was increasingly clear that private landlords could not be relied on to improve the dreadful conditions of disrepair, overcrowding, and shared kitchens, bathrooms and toilets.

The Kensington Housing Trust was highly regarded by almost all Councillors. This is demonstrated graphically in research carried out by John Dearlove, a political scientist from Sussex University who carried out an in-depth study of views of local organisations held by Kensington and Chelsea councillors. The Kensington Housing Trust was seen as helpful by significantly more councillors than any other organisation. In stark contrast the other organisations working in North Kensington (the North Kensington Playspace Group, the North Kensington Family Study, the Notting Hill Social Council and the Neighbourhood Service Unit) all came close to the bottom of the list. (The Notting Hill Housing Trust is not listed as it was not included in the sample).

Although the publicity and fundraising of the Notting Hill Housing Trust's launch had given it a high profile, its day-to-day work was the low-key activity of buying, renovating and letting individual houses. Relationships were being built up with Council officials, but there was little contact with the key councillors.

By 1969, however, the Trust had strengthened its reputation for delivering a growing housing programme. John Coward had built up relationships with both councillors and council officers. Whilst the Trust's position was clear on the urgent need for much stronger intervention by the Council in North Kensington, it had avoided making public criticisms.

On 24 June the Council held a press conference to announce its new policies. Although it publicly rejected the attacks on its record, the barrage of criticism was finally influencing the policies of the local authority.

The new approach outlined by Sir Malby Crofton was markedly different from previous policies. He no longer tried to justify the slow and ineffective clearance programme. He spoke of the need for *"clearance and improvement activity to preserve the character of the local community"*. Previously the Council had been indifferent to the activity of developers who forced low income tenants out of the area. Most significantly of all Crofton spoke of a *"significant change of ownership from private to other hands"*.

To achieve this *"change of ownership"* the Council introduced a uniquely generous form of financial subsidy for housing associations. Under this scheme the Council met in full the annual revenue deficit on all the properties purchased to house tenants living in the borough.

The difficulty that the Trust had been facing was that spiralling housing costs were squeezing them out of the market. Although it had been receiving subsidies from the Government and the Council to reduce the cost of repaying loans, these had not been high enough where the cost of purchase and renovation were expensive. The new policy was intended to enable the Trust to pay market prices and still provide homes for low income tenants.

Since its early days the Trust had relied on the Greater London Council scheme for funding its development work. This was generous by the standards of most local authority arrangements, but still left a deficit on many projects. The new Kensington and Chelsea scheme was the most generous scheme of help to housing associations given by any local authority. In this key principle it presaged the changes in the subsequent 1974 Housing Act, which would transform the financial framework for housing associations.

Shortly afterwards the Council announced its new policies for tackling housing problems in the Golborne and Colville area, which was where the worst problems of overcrowding, multi-occupation and poor housing conditions were concentrated.

In the Golborne ward, the Council decided that redevelopment was the most appropriate option for most of the area, given the age and condition of most of the properties. The Greater London Council was asked to carry out the redevelopment of the Swinbrook Road area, between the Portobello Road and the motorway. The Kensington Housing Trust was given the responsibility for the Murchison and Wheatstone Road areas, between Portobello Road and Ladbroke Grove.

Notting Hill Housing Trust was given responsibility for the Colville/Tavistock area. This was bounded by the District tube line in the north, Ladbroke Grove to the west, the boundary with Westminster to the east, and Westbourne Grove in the south. In total this area contained 1100 properties, of which 15% were already owned by either the local authority or a housing association. The Trust was asked to take on a rolling programme of acquisition and conversion of properties in the Colville and Tavistock area, to the south of motorway and railway. This area was in the heart of North Kensington, comprising mostly large three or four storey terraced houses, and was known to contain many of the worst problems in the area.

In recent years some properties had been converted into flats for sale, such as the development at 1-9 Colville Gardens, But the majority were still owned by private landlords. Since the 1965 Rent Act there had been a growth of furnished tenancies, let at higher rents, with very limited security of tenure. Almost all were multi-occupied with tenants sharing bathrooms and toilets. Many were in poor repair with high levels of overcrowding.

The Trust's view was that the problems and potential of the Colville/Tavistock area had no counterpart anywhere else in the country, and therefore original solutions needed to be found. Many residents experienced severe housing problems, yet there was also strong market demand for properties from more affluent newcomers. The challenge was to find ways of removing deprivation without the removal of the existing community.

During 1970 the Trust succeeded in buying 36 houses containing 136 tenancies, with almost all of the properties being wholly or partly occupied. The problem was that few properties were coming on to the market. In the absence of any compulsory powers landlords owning sub-standard properties could continue making a good return. They did this by letting furnished tenancies at high rents to low income tenants, who had no other choice. Where properties were put on the market they were being bought up by speculative developers with whom the Trust could not compete.

The community groups became more and more angry as they saw developers outbidding the Trust at property auctions. The People's Association Housing Group decided on a new tactic. When 25 Powis Square was put up for auction about a dozen of its members went along to the London Auction Mart.

When Lot 32, 25 Powis Square, was reached, the bidding started at £17,000 and two other people followed by making bids. However, when the offers reached £23,000, members of the People' Association started bidding too. They raised their newspapers and cocked the forefingers just like the regular auction goers. Soon they were on their own, as the early bidders dropped out. Higher and higher went the bids, and angrier and angrier the other bidders became. *"They're playing games"* one shouted. *"How childish"* cried another. When £35,000 was reached the auctioneer stopped the bidding. Addressing the last bidder he said *"I have reason to believe you are not worth £35,000"*. After hurried consultations he announced that he was selling the property for £21,000 to the earlier bidder, and not taking any more bids. The price was £1,000 more than the Notting Hill Housing Trust was able to pay.

A year later, however, 25 Powis Square came up for auction again, this time at the Cumberland Hotel. Shortly after proceedings were due to start, the auctioneer apologized for the delay in starting, which he said was caused by the presence of some *"people called squatters – undesirable elements that should be eliminated from our society"*. He then held up a document which had been distributed by two young women, headed "Supplementary Particulars", and told everyone to ignore it since it was *"a pack of lies"*. However, most of those present had already been reading it with some interest, as the information it contained was clearly relevant to any potential buyers.

Set out in the format of an estate agent's particulars, it detailed the conditions of each floor:

"Supplementary particulars
25 Powis Square

Situated on the corner of Powis Square (where political demonstrations, affrays and rioting are frequent occurrences) in a noisy, unstable, multi-racial, high crime area.

Top floor: *Superficially redecorated. New electric fixtures over faulty wiring. Damp already well apparent...*

2nd floor: *Faulty wiring. Damp. Regulated unfurnished tenancy, occupied by a family with children...*

1st floor: *Extensive area of woodworm and dry rot in the structural timbers. Portico structurally unsound. Serious damp affecting exterior wall...*

Grnd floor :   *No repairs have been done for 40 years. Rodent infestation. Extensive replastering required...*

Basement: *Extensive damp. No damp course. Faulty wiring"*

Whilst potential bidders were digesting this information, the buyer for the Notting Hill Housing Trust rushed up to the auctioneer with the owner of 25 Powis Square. Negotiations went on for several minutes, and then the auctioneer announced that the property had been sold to the Trust. A great cheer went up, albeit only from some of those present.

In fact, it was not a coincidence that the intervention by members of the People's Association helped the Trust to buy the property. In advance of auctions the Trust's property buyer, Adrian Maynard, was secretly tipping off leading members of the People's Association on houses he hoped to buy and informing them of the highest price the Trust could bid.

The People's Association members only started to bid when the Trust's buyer had reached the limit of what he could offer. When all other bidders dropped out, the "bogus" bidders took it in turn to make new offers, until the auctioneer realized what was happening and stopped the auction.

As Jan O'Malley explains: *"It was really quite frightening, as everyone had to remember when to bid. If somebody forgot, or nipped off to the toilet, the auctioneer could declare the property sold to the last person to bid, who would be liable for 10% of the offer. Fortunately nobody ever did."*

A further difficulty for the Trust was the result of uncertainty over the Council's long term plans for some parts of the area, so that it was not possible to carry out full-scale rehabilitation. The Trust were not privy to plans being prepared by the Council's Planning department, even though it was the main agency carrying out physical improvements in the area. It believed that it had a duty to its own tenants to ensure they had a say on the future of the neighbourhood in which they lived.

In December 1970 a meeting was held between members of the Trust's committee and senior officers with the Chairmen and Vice-chairmen of Council committees. As a result of this the Trust was asked to formulate proposals on how the Council should embark on a comprehensive planning and action study of the whole Colville/Tavistock area.

The proposals prepared by the Trust were submitted to a further meeting between representatives of the Trust and the Council in March 1971, chaired by Sir Malby Crofton. The Trust's proposals outlined the scope of issues that a study should cover. These were to establish the physical requirements of the area, in terms of the number of houses, their condition, size and tenure, but also of schools, shops, local industry and community facilities; to assess the financial implications of proposals for rehabilitation and of any areas where redevelopment was considered appropriate; and the arrangements for public consultation. In view of the Trust's major stake in improving the area, it was also proposed that a special team should be set up to carry out the study, and this should report to a joint committee of the Council and the Trust.

The outcome of the meeting was the setting up a joint working party to consider the Trust's proposals and submit recommendations to the Council. Following this, several meetings were held and joint recommendations were submitted to the Council's Board of Management.

In key respects these recommendations followed the Trust's proposals for the scope of the study and the establishment of a joint steering committee. The study should be completed in nine months. A director and team of 14 staff was proposed, although some of the posts would be for less than the full period of the study. The Trust would make available a property in the area as an office for the study team. The total cost was estimated to be £31,370.

Following the submission of these proposals the Trust heard nothing for five months, despite a letter to the Leader of the Council in August. Eventually, a meeting was held between John Coward and the Town Clerk, together with senior council officials. At this meeting it emerged that the Council's plans for carrying out the proposed study were significantly different from the proposals of the working party.

Leading appointments to the team had been made without any consultation with the Trust. The specialist posts for studying the social needs of the community had been deleted. Very little importance was given to consultation with local people. The Council had dropped plans for a joint steering committee with representatives of the Trust. Under the Council proposals the Trust's direct role was limited to making available a vacant property in the area as a local office for the study team.

On 7 November members of the Trust committee and John Coward met with Sir Malby Crofton and John Webber, the Town Clerk. They expressed serious disappointment at the Council's plans, especially the omission of the earlier proposals for publicising the work of the study and consulting with local residents. They warned that this would lead to adverse criticism, especially since some community groups were already very suspicious of the Council's intentions for the study.

The Trust no longer felt it could make available an office, as previously offered. The only reason the Trust had been willing to offer the use of a property, which would otherwise have been used for residential accommodation, was to enable the study team to have close and regular contact with local residents. The Council no longer seemed to see this as a priority. The Trust's representatives went to the meeting with the firm view that unless the Council changed their plans, the Trust would disassociate itself from involvement in the study.

Faced by such strong criticism from its potential partner in the study, and the lead housing association for the area, the Council leadership agreed to revise the plans again, by publicizing the study and consulting with local residents more extensively. As a result, the Trust representatives agreed to support the study and to make available a property for use as an office. However, they still had misgiving about the Council's intentions.

In order to make clear its own views on the future of the Colville/Tavistock area the Trust produced its own report in October 1972 setting out what it saw as the key issues for the study. The key recommendations were that:

"At least 60% of the residential properties in Colville/Tavistock should be transferred from private into public ownership;

The Council should resolve to compulsorily purchase all properties which are to be transferred from private to public ownership;

The Council should give a firm commitment to retain or rehouse all those residents who wish to remain in the area".

To carry out the study, the Council appointed Frank Clinch, the Director of Technical Services. His appointment was greeted with considerable scepticism by community organisations in North Kensington. He had previously been the Municipal Engineer, and had no background of working in housing. They believed that he had been appointed to do the bidding of the Council's leadership, and would not make recommendations for any radical changes in policy. In this, however, they would prove mistaken.

Frank Clinch set up his offices in St Luke's Road, in the heart of the Tavistock area, and announced his intention to consult widely with local residents. However, the People's Association and other organisations decided not to co-operate with the study and to boycott the Community Forum that was set up.

After the first Community Forum was attended by only 50 people, the People's Association Housing Group called its own Action Meeting. It had two aims: to say "NO" to the study and to make the area a "NO GO" zone for property speculators. The Kensington Post reported on 28 July 1972 that:

"More than 300 people, young and old, militant and not-so-militant responding to the People's Association call to 'act now' met in the All Saint's Church Hall. The Housing Group succeeded where the Borough Council and the Housing Trust have failed – they got the people of Colville to tell them what they wanted for the area in line with the Housing Group's demands. Single people, old age pensioners, mothers with children gave first hand experiences of pressures, inducements and harassment…. The momentum of their resentment and determination to fight for their homes overwhelmed the meeting".

In her book "The Politics of Community Action", Jan O'Malley recalls that the Housing Group was amazed by the strength and unity of the meeting, but comments that this was not achieved by chance:

"For weeks before the Housing Group established a full-scale presence on the streets, distributing thousands of copies of the 'People's News' special issue, explaining the background to the battle in housing and all about the Colville study".

The most dramatic confrontation came at the next meeting of the Community Forum. In order to demonstrate the strength of feeling by local people, the Housing Group had decided to urge people to attend this meeting. Before the Council representatives arrived the hall was packed out and people had to stand outside looking through the open windows.

After Councillor John Methuen, Chair of the Housing Committee, had explained the new policy on improvement grants there was an angry response on the lack of checks to prevent speculators buying properties and tenants being evicted. At this point the Housing Group introduced their own "alternative agenda" to consider their own proposals, but Rev. Peter Clarke who was chairing the meeting refused to accept it and tried to close the meeting. Whereupon, the People's News reported:

"All the dignitaries made a rush for the door – only to find the doors locked and people blocking their path. One by one they were confronted and tackled by people from the audience. Clinch and Methuen anxiously tried to unbolt the door behind the audience, but it wouldn't budge. Seeing there was no possible escape for them, they had to return to their seats and listen to what the people wanted".

The "People's Agenda" included resolutions that the Council must give a written guarantee to residents that they would be able to stay in the area in improved homes at low rents; that private landlords be eliminated from the area since they had proved themselves incapable of providing decent homes at low rents; and that the Council must start the compulsory purchase of every badly managed house immediately. Council representatives were eventually allowed to leave at 10.20 pm. Not surprisingly the Council decided to cancel future Community Forums.

When the report of the study was published in February 1973, however, it confounded the predictions of those who had seen Frank Clinch's appointment as a whitewash. John Coward's assessment is that *"after moving into the area he had gone native"*.

The report explained in detail how improvements by private landlords were forcing local people out of the area. Using an example of a typical 4 storey house, it calculated that the average cost rent charged by a landlord for a converted flat would be £25 a week, whilst the housing association rent would be £13. It looked at these rents in the context of the income levels of the present population, and found that *"even for the 11% of the population with income of over £40 a week the rent of £25 would be virtually impossible"*.

The key conclusion of the Report was that *"private improvement must result in a complete change in the social structure of the neighbourhood and would rob the Colville/Tavistock area of its traditional role in the community, providing homes for unskilled and semi-skilled manual workers"*. The policy advocated for the area was for the *"Council to use such powers as it had to secure that, wherever possible, terraces pass into the ownership of the Council or a housing trust as a whole, and that it should compulsorily purchase immediately the 450 houses in the area which were multi-occupied and unconverted, so as to protect the residents from the activities of speculators"*.

The front-page headline in the Kensington Post was *"The Clinch Report: Colville's new deal"*. The Post went on to report its key recommendation that *"the Council should make massive use of its compulsory purchase powers in the Colville/Tavistock area to buy decaying houses for conversion into decent homes, either for sale or rent"*.

Following the publication of the report, a coalition of organisations, including the Notting Hill Housing Trust, the Social Council and the People's Association, came together to agree proposals to the Council on the basis of the findings of the Study. As a result seven major recommendations were put to the Council, including the compulsory purchase of all privately rented properties, unless the owners showed they were willing to improve them and let them at affordable rents.

When the Council met in July 1973 the recommendations did not endorse in full the recommendations of the Clinch Report or the coalition of community organisations. The critical difference was that the Council proposed only to use its CPO powers on individual properties where the owner had failed to remedy poor conditions. However, it endorsed the policy of seeking the transfer of ownership to the Notting Hill Housing Trust in order to provide improved homes at rents affordable to existing residents.

Much of the local drama had taken place against the wider background of social unrest which culminated in the miners' strike and fall of Edward Heath's Conservative government in February 1974. But a strong degree of bipartisanship prevailed over housing issues that affected North Kensington. Following the passing of the 1974 Housing Act, a Tory measure adopted by the incoming Labour government, the Colville/Tavistock area was declared as the first Housing Action Area (HAA) in the country.

The Act followed a White Paper "Better Homes: the new priorities" which had been published by the Heath Government in June 1973, four months after the publication of the Clinch Report.

The White Paper's description of the criteria which made an area suitable for an HAA could hardly have been closer to the characteristics of the Colville/Tavistock area. These included both housing and social factors, including:

- Households living at a density exceeding 1.5 persons per room.
- Furnished tenancies.
- Shared accommodation.
- Elderly people and large families.
- Houses lacking a large water supply, a fixed bath or an inside WC.

Within Housing Action Areas the White Paper said the Government would *"be prepared to look sympathetically on the use of existing compulsory purchase powers"*. It also proposed new powers to:

- Empower local authorities to compel minimum standards of improvement.
- Give local authorities powers to impose conditions on the payment of grants to landlords to ensure that rented accommodation was kept available for letting at registered rents.
- Empower local authorities to require landlords selling tenanted property to offer first refusal of the sale of the property to an approved housing association; or if this was shown to be impracticable, to the local authority itself.
- Place local authorities under a statutory duty to re-house any tenant temporarily or permanently displaced from accommodation.

The whole approach of the White Paper marked a radical shift in Government policy towards improving older property. Previous policies had relied almost entirely on encouraging voluntary improvement by private owners. The new policy recognised that in many areas of severe housing stress, especially in inner London, properties should be transferred to social ownership, and that compulsory powers would be needed where existing owners would not improve their properties for the benefit of existing residents.

---

1. *Report of the Milner Holland Committee on Housing in Greater London, 1965.*

Chapter 6

TAKING STOCK

Between 1966 and 1973 there had been a sustained campaign by community organisations for new housing policies in North Kensington. They believed that the Borough Council had wilfully neglected the intolerable housing problems in the area. The members of the community organisations believed that policy changes would not be achieved without hard-hitting reports, public meetings, media publicity and, on occasions, direct action. They were physically close to the BBC Television Centre at Wood Lane and had good contacts at what were then London's two evening papers, especially the sophisticated Evening Standard which was read by policymakers. It all helped.

However, the leading community activists also developed a complex analysis of how political influence could be achieved, which became more sophisticated over time. Whilst believing in open and participative forms of action, they recognised that considerable power was wielded by public bodies, especially by Kensington and Chelsea Council. Despite the rhetoric of "community power", campaigning groups could only achieve their goals by persuasion. Crucial to this was developing alliances with individuals and agencies who were in a position to influence decisions.

Political power in Kensington and Chelsea Council rested firmly with the Conservative Party. The Tories had held unbroken control for many years, and barring a political earthquake, seemed certain to retain it for the foreseeable future. Within the Conservative Party a great deal of power was held by the Leader, and a small inner group of leading councillors. Senior officers had less influence on policies than in many local authorities, but were then given authority to implement them without interference.

The critical turning points in housing policy were Sir Malby Crofton's decision to adopt a new housing strategy in the summer of 1969, followed four years later by the decision on the renewal strategy for the Colville/Tavistock area. Whilst the Council never publicly renounced the old policies, the new strategy effectively abandoned the belief that private landlords would provide decent, rented homes at rents affordable by low income tenants.

However, the Council leadership was not prepared to adopt the policy of some Labour-controlled authorities in London, and entrust its housing department with the task of acquiring and renovating privately owned houses. Instead, as we have seen, responsibility was given to two housing associations, with the GLC being asked to undertake a substantial new redevelopment area in the Golborne Road.

The Notting Hill Housing Trust found itself in a sensitive position. Unlike the other housing associations it had spoken out against the scandal of poor housing conditions in the area ever since it had been formed. The policies which the Trust called on the Council to adopt were almost identical to key demands of the community organisations. Yet the Trust also recognised that housing associations had a special role as agencies which were capable of carrying out the necessary improvement work. This vital goal could only be achieved by gaining the confidence and trust of the local authority.

The key contact between the Trust and the Council was John Coward. Himself a former council housing manager, he managed over several years to build up strong relationships of trust, initially with senior officers of the Council, and then with leading councillors. There were sharp disagreements at times, such as the threat to pull out of the Colville/Tavistock study. The Trust consistently pressed the Council to take stronger action, especially on the need to use compulsory purchase powers. Yet it did not join the public protests that came from the community.

John also kept in close contact with people in the community organisations, especially John and Jan O'Malley. Their radical style of community action was new to him. Unsurprisingly, he had never experienced anything like it in all his years as a housing manager. By nature his style is to seek results by quiet diplomacy rather than public campaigning, but he respected those who had chosen a different way of seeking to achieve change.

As John Coward explains: *"I got on extremely well with the O'Malleys, even though they were giving me a very hard time. If I had a problem I went round to see them. They actually helped quite a lot with my education. I came an awfully long way to see their point of view, even though the Trust had a different role to play"*.

The 1960s and early 1970s were tumultuous years in North Kensington, marked by an extraordinary outburst of community activity. It started with the new groups formed following the racial disturbances and the death of Kelso Cochrane. These included the Colville and Powis tenants' organisation, the Methodist Group ministry and the New Left group.

Then came the creation of the Social Council, the birth of Notting Hill Housing Trust, the first Notting Hill Carnival, the setting up of the Notting

Hill Community Workshop, the formation of the People's Association, the creation of the Motorway Development Group and the 1967 Summer Project, with its Housing Survey, Neighbourhood Advice Centres and summer play schemes.

For many years the people of Notting Hill had experienced a feeling of powerlessness. Their homes were owned by absentee landlords. Decisions on plans for their area were made by councillors they never saw or met. Homes were torn down to make way for the Westway, a flyover section of motorway which proved to be the first (and only) section of the inner London motorway box. Protests elsewhere, not least in more expensive parts of Kensington south of the Shepherd's Bush roundabout, led to the wider project's abandonment. Across North Kensington the Westway left a gaping hole in the middle of the community: another symbol of its powerlessness. There were others. Even the garden squares were locked by invisible owners, denying local children anywhere safe to play.

One of the most important aims of community action was to win back control for residents in the area, and this was expressed in a range of the campaigns and new initiatives which were launched.

The Notting Hill Carnival was a unique event where the black community could visibly celebrate in the streets. This developed enormous symbolic importance, especially for young black people who often experienced life on the streets as places which were threatening and unsafe. As it grew annually in size, it developed into the largest street festival in Europe and a unique multi-racial social event with special importance for the Afro-Caribbean community across the capital and beyond.

The North Kensington Amenity Trust fought to reclaim the land under the Westway for community use. The building of the motorway had been planned and implemented at rooftop level with virtually no consultation with the local community. Hundreds of residents had been displaced from their homes, with homes, shops and businesses demolished to make space for this huge elevated dual carriage way cutting through the heart of North Kensington.

There had been plans for using the space under the motorway for car parking and a bus garage, but there had been no publicity or consultation over any of the plans. By promoting ideas - with maps, diagrams and photos - about how the space might be used, the Amenity Trust had opened a discussion of what possible uses might be. These developed into an ambitious new community business, which combined space for play areas, nursery centres, shops, meeting areas, offices for voluntary organisations and commercial businesses. Success gradually provided another symbol that the community could fight back.

Demonstrations by local mothers over the dangers of traffic in busy streets had highlighted the lack of safe places for children to play, and led to the creation of play streets and summer play schemes. What many local people saw as most insulting was the scandal of the locked gardens in Powis and Colville Square, where absentee owners kept fencing around the empty squares in order to stop their use by local residents. After years of protest and campaigning, the pulling down of the fences was celebrated as another huge community victory.

Most vital of all for people in North Kensington was having somewhere secure to live, without fear of harassment or eviction. If the future of North Kensington had been left to the working of market forces, most of the poor would have been forced out, especially in the areas being gentrified. All the attractive properties up for sale would have been bought up by the speculative developers and occupied by affluent incomers, the sort of people who would one day be depicted in the film "Notting Hill" which is regrettably notable for the absence of non-white faces.

The housing campaigns enabled low income residents to stay in North Kensington and to live in the homes that were modernized. The activity of the Notting Hill Housing Trust was critical in preserving streets with a mix of housing tenures, lived in by people with different backgrounds, incomes and ethnic origins. It remains part of the neighbourhood's attraction – even for yuppies.

All these campaigns were means through which people living and working in North Kensington gained control over what took place in their community. They were empowered by different ways of gaining access to, or recovering space. Through these different ways, people gained self-confidence, learning different ways of working together and how to achieve their goals.

To its credit the Borough Council abandoned the "siege mentality" which marked its initial reaction to the mounting barrage of criticism, especially of its housing record. Key roles were played by Sir Malby Crofton, and a small group of younger, "modernising" Conservative councillors representing wards in North Kensington.

What took place was a virtual transformation of the Council's housing strategy in North Kensington. The belief that private landlords would provide decent accommodation for low income residents was abandoned. Housing associations were given the leading role in carrying out comprehensive plans for either redevelopment or rehabilitation.

There are different views on why and how this transformation took place. Almost undeniably it was the result of action by a range of different individuals and agencies, with some frequently in conflict but eventually coming close to agreement.

There was universal agreement, however, that the Trust played a pivotal role. Whilst it had no mandate to decide on policies for the area, it gained legitimacy from its practical activity of buying and renovating houses and providing homes for local people. This experience also gave it a growing bank of knowledge and expertise, which informed its policy proposals.

With the Council determined not to carry out redevelopment or rehabilitation itself, the Notting Hill and Kensington Housing Trusts provided an alternative route, which was also acceptable to the community organisations.

Looking back on the first ten years

The Trust's annual report in September 1973 looks back at what had been achieved in its first ten years. Over the time the number of properties bought each year had grown steadily, with the exception of the fall in 1972 which reflected the rise in prices in the housing market during that period:

1964	5
1965	17
1966	32
1967	46
1968	37
1969	65
1970	114
1971	146
1972	87
1973	162

At the end of 1973 the Trust's reached its 10th anniversary. Its annual report welcomed the fact that: *"both political parties were in fundamental agreement on an analysis of housing in stress areas which is very similar to that expressed by the Trust in its previous annual reports"*. This was a very different position to that in the early 1960s when the political parties still saw solutions in large scale redevelopment programmes, and there was little understanding of the housing problems faced in areas like Notting Hill.

The report went on: *"If the Trust had existed only in order to bring attention to bear on housing stress it would be satisfying enough to recognize this approach in a new Housing Bill. But the Trust's energies have been primarily concentrated during these ten years at a practical level. In that time it has secured 2,000 homes which would not otherwise have been provided. To achieve this the Trust has had to take the lead in forging changes in the structure of statutory housing finance which provided such an obstacle in the Trust's early days."*

It was a fitting recognition that John Coward was awarded the OBE in the New Years Honours List in 1974.

Looking back on the achievements of the Trust in its first ten years they were incredible. It had acquired properties to provide over 2,000 flats, and let them to low income families in severe housing need. At the start this had been done without any adequate statutory framework of financial assistance, in the face of a gap between development costs and rental income.

It had expanded its activities from North Kensington into acquiring and renovating properties in the neighbouring borough of Hammersmith and Fulham. It had played a leading role in persuading the Borough Council to abandon its neglect of the housing problems of North Kensington and support an ambitious and innovative programme of housing development and renovation, with the Trust as the major partner and agency.

In addition to all this, it was working in one of the most difficult areas of housing stress in the country, carrying out the most hazardous kind of housing renovation. And it had done this working in a highly charged, racially diverse community, where there were conflicting views of how best to achieve progressive change. The Trust had come a long way since setting up its market stall in the Portobello Road ten years before.

The Trust had become a recognised leader of the new wave of charitable housing associations, rehabilitating older properties in inner city areas of housing stress. It had played the leading role in the launch of Shelter, which for several years was a vital line in providing funding for newly formed associations.

It had been a key player in persuading the Government to create a new funding regime which would pave the way for a massive expansion of housing association activity. The next chapter describes the role that the Trust played, especially through John Coward, in influencing Government policies which would lead to a new legal and financial framework for housing associations.

In 1973 Michael White wrote a leaflet which summed up the progress the Trust had made over its first ten years in an anniversary brochure. It sums up the sense of achievement the Trust had for what it had achieved, but also the anger at the conditions people still had to endure, and the urgency of finding solutions.

"*We don't pretend to have solved the housing problems of one corner of London. Or even that we ever could.*

What we can do as we approach our tenth anniversary is point to 2,000 homes owned by the Notting Hill Housing Trust and ask 'What would have happened to the 5,000 people who live in them if the Trust hadn't been around?'

Probably some would have managed on their own. If they had been really lucky they might have got a council flat. But most would have had to struggle on as best they could. Old people, large families, living in damp, decaying and overcrowded rooms, paying too much rent, and always with the fear of eviction and homelessness hanging over them. The Trust has given them the lucky break they needed, a decent home, a reasonable rent, security, a chance to make a go of life, which the Trust has given to more than 5000 people since it was founded in 1963.

You may remember 1963. It was the year the public first heard of Peter Rachman and his ruthless slum landlord activities in Notting Hill. The Trust was founded in the wake of the outcry against 'Rachmanism'.

In its first year it bought just five properties. Last year it acquired almost three a week.

We've all come a long way since then. Public understanding of homelessness and bad housing is better than ever before. People appreciate how difficult it is to escape once you've been sucked down into the vicious poverty cycle.

But if public understanding has grown, so have the problems. It's always been a race against the clock, and it's getting faster all the time. That's why the Trust is launching a special appeal for funds to mark its tenth anniversary in 1973. YOUR help is needed more than ever before. Just listen…

The basic reason why there is more homelessness, despite all that's been done, is that the number of homes available for low income families to rent is dwindling fast. Slums are being pulled down, but expensive homes or office blocks or motorways are going up in their place. A hostel is demolished and is replaced by a hotel. Most dramatic of all is the rise in house prices, which has made it worthwhile to property developers to move into 'twilight areas' like Notting Hill. Suddenly last year's slum property can be snapped up and turned into next year's luxury flat.

And all too often the Trust loses both ways. The developer (he's got more money) gets the property, and the Trust gets the evicted tenants on its doorstep. More tenants to house, fewer houses to put them in.

The Trust is holding its own, but even when it can buy property and house people the problems aren't over. Other pressures in our society, unemployment, the cost of living, the bewildering pace of modern life, all of which hit the poor hardest, end up at the Trust's door.

Can you imagine a family so battered by years in a single slum room that it has to be coaxed into using all three rooms in its new Trust flat? Well it has happened. And the Trust gives welfare support and advice to those tenants who need it to get back on their feet.

It may be furniture at a bargain price, or help with laying lino, advice about family allowance benefit, special equipment for the old or disabled, a rent rebate, or the occasional baby-sitter for the unsupported mother.

All this the Trust can provide because of the time given by its many volunteer workers, and the money and gifts from its other supporters. It is vital that this work continues".

Chapter 7

INFLUENCING
NATIONAL POLICIES

During the late 1960s and early 1970s the changes in Notting Hill began to be matched by important developments at the national level. By the start of the 1970s the new inner city based housing associations were making an impact across the country, especially in Liverpool, Birmingham, Manchester and inner London boroughs. However, they lacked the channels for making their voices heard at the national level.

The National Federation of Housing Societies (NFHS) was the recognised representative body for housing associations. It had been created in 1935 and by 1961 it had a total of 671 members. The 1961 Act gave a strong boost to the growth of housing associations, with the Government setting up a loan fund for lending to housing associations providing "cost rent" accommodation. This was intended to extend provision for middle income households, without any public subsidy. The 1964 Housing Act gave a further boost, with the creation of the Housing Corporation as the body to channel funds for cost rent and co-ownership housing.

As well as the cost rent and co-ownership societies, a large number of specialist housing associations for older people were set up in the 1960s. As a result, by 1969 the NFHS had 1,945 members, including a small number of old philanthropic trusts, 595 old people's associations, 436 cost rent and co-ownership associations and 198 self-build associations.

During the 1960s a number of new associations were set up by professionals whose main purpose was to earn fees from carrying out the architectural, surveying or legal work of development activity. These associations had become the dominant force in the NFHS. They were eligible for the same loans and subsidies as the charitable housing associations. But their motives were very different, as were their priorities for new legislation.

The charitable housing associations engaged in rehabilitating older property in inner city areas became frustrated that almost all the work of the NFHS was devoted to representing the cost rent and new build societies and that it was not effectively representing their interests.

In the late 1960s a small group of London associations, including the Notting Hill Housing Trust, decided action was needed. Sometimes referred to as "the plotters", they met usually in the offices of Father Paul Byrne at the Shelter Housing Aid Centre (SHAC) - and began to map out the changes they saw were needed.

As a first step they set up the London Housing Association Committee (LHAC) outside the NFHS. One of LHAC's roles was to liaise with the Greater London Council, which had become a large scale funder of housing association activity, especially where the borough councils were not willing to help. LHAC also took on a wider role in representing the interests of the inner London rehabilitation associations to Government.

The Chair of LHAC was Anthony Fletcher, the Director of London and Quadrant Housing Trust. He had been a Conservative member of the GLC from 1965 to 1968. He had also worked previously in Edward Heath's private office and had a range of valuable political contacts. Whilst John Coward was the quiet persuader, Anthony Fletcher was the more flamboyant advocate. Their combined skills made LHAC a very effective lobbying organisation.

At a later stage the Improvement Action Committee was set up within the NFHS, to represent the interests of the inner city associations from different areas of the country at a national level. This was chaired by John Coward and became a key vehicle for developing and communicating policy proposals for housing association rehabilitation activity.

In the early 1970s, the Conservative Government was giving increasing attention to the need for more effective policies both for inner city renovation and for promoting the role of housing associations as a "third arm" in housing provision. Successive Secretaries of State for the Environment, Peter Walker and Geoffrey Rippon, publicly set out this new policy direction. It was also strongly promoted by the Housing Minister, Paul Channon, who had a personal involvement with housing associations through having been a Board member of the Guinness Trust for ten years. Channon was a member of the Guinness family, son of the famous diarist MP, Chips Channon, and his heiress wife, Honor. As a baby in 1936 he had tried to pull off Queen Mary's earrings.

A critical disagreement between the different types of associations was over the standards required from those receiving public subsidy. The associations which had committee members earning fees from their work were strongly opposed to any proposals to ban this. The charitable associations believed that preventing committee members from earning fees was essential. Only by banning this practice could housing associations secure political and public support for the growth of housing association activity.

The tensions came to a head at the Annual Conference of the NFHS, held over a weekend at Warwick University in September 1972. The Government was known to be considering new housing legislation, including major changes which would affect housing associations. At breakfast on the Sunday morning of the conference, delegates were given the policy document which the Council was proposing to submit to the Department of the Environment. To the dismay of the progressive associations it was a very complacent document, which fudged the issue of conflicts of interest of committee members.

Six delegates, including John Coward and Ken Bartlett, the Director of Paddington Churches Housing Association, were so outraged by this document that they decided to make a joint protest. As soon as the morning conference session started, they stood up to speak, one after another, to criticise the draft document.

The Chair of the NFHS was Lewis Waddilove, the Director of the Joseph Rowntree Foundation. He had many years of experience in the voluntary housing movement and was widely respected. He believed the newly formed associations had a key role in tackling the housing problems in inner city areas. Sensing the need to respond to the unexpectedly strong criticisms of the draft document, he proposed that those who took that view should leave the session and come back with their alternative proposals. To the surprise of everyone present, around eighty of the two hundred delegates stood up and left the hall with the small group who had spoken.

The "walk out" – as it became known – was a very visible sign of the unhappiness of a significant number of members with the policy stance of the NFHS. Its importance was that these members included almost all the "new wave" of associations. They were the associations with the highest public profile and credibility with both local authorities and central government. They were increasingly being seen as key players in new policies for urban regeneration and in breaking the monopoly of local authorities as the only providers of socially rented housing.

The open rift at the Warwick conference persuaded Lewis Waddilove that changes were needed. Shortly afterwards, he convened an informal two day meeting in York of representatives from the main inner city associations. John Coward believes that this meeting was critical in developing a worked out and coherent set of policy proposals.

Another important change was the resignation of Geoffrey Hall, the Director of the NFHS. In May 1973 he was replaced by Richard Best, the Director of the British Churches Housing Trust, who was closely associated with the inner city associations. He had been the Secretary of LHAC and then became the Secretary of the Improvement Action Committee in the NFHS.

At the annual meeting of the NFHS in May 1973 Lewis Waddilove stood down, having served his full term of office. The two candidates standing to replace him were Anthony Fletcher, the Director of the London and Quadrant Housing Trust, and Alderman Fieldhouse, who ran a group of fee-earning housing associations in Manchester. They represented the two wings of the NFHS, and the vote was seen as crucial for its future direction.

However, the vote resulted in a tie, with Lewis Waddilove entitled as the Chair to have the casting vote. His response was characteristic of his Quaker beliefs and philosophy. After a few moments thought he announced that he wanted to have time to consider the situation, and would come to the next meeting of the Council with his proposal.

The "solution" he devised was to find a new candidate, who he hoped would be seen as independent of the different groups and able to act as a unifying influence. The person he identified was Raymond Hylton, a member of the House of Lords, who had a close involvement with housing associations through his involvement with the Catholic Housing Aid Society. His nomination was accepted by the Council, and an open rift avoided.

The outcome of these events was very significant. Despite the valuable contribution housing associations had made in local areas, they had been seen as marginal to national housing policies. The NFHS had never achieved a public profile outside its own membership.

By the early 1970s this had started to change, mainly as a result of the work of the inner city associations. The new leadership in the NFHS was crucial in strengthening confidence in the role housing associations could play, especially with Government.

One important element in achieving this was the alliance that developed between the older charitable trusts - especially the Peabody, Guinness and William Sutton Trusts - and the new generation of charitable associations. In the post-war years the older trusts had carried out very little new development.

Seeing the new opportunities for charitable associations – the older trusts began meeting together to look at the legislative and policy changes they wanted to see. Fortuitously Paul Channon, then Housing Minister, was very supportive of the role that housing associations could play. This provided these older trusts with valuable access to the DoE's policy making.

They recognised that it was not the cost rent and co-ownership societies, but the new generation of charitable, inner city associations who were their key allies – and John Coward became an important link. They recognised in him a deceptively soft-spoken but experienced housing professional with a proven track record, who had achieved results in one of the toughest neighbourhoods in the country.

The alliance between the various strands in the housing association movement was important in developing a powerful coalition. Richard Best believes that:

"The Notting Hill Housing Trust helped transform provision of housing for those on lower incomes. Creating a ginger group within an established structure, and generating a synergy between key players gave the messages from Notting Hill a much wider resonance.

By bringing together not only a handful of the new generation of housing associations in 'the twilight areas' group (Paddington Churches, the Family Housing Associations, Quadrant Housing Trust, New Islington and Hackney Housing Association and others), but also the earlier predecessors run by a new generation (Copec in Birmingham, Liverpool Improved Houses), Notting Hill was able to help change radically the collective structures of the National Federation. Through the pressure group within the Improvement Action Committee, and the external impetus from the London Housing Association Council, the national body became something very different."

The different types of charitable associations took on the leadership of the NFHS – now re-naming itself as the National Federation of Housing Associations. With Richard Best installed as Director, it became a highly effective lobbying organisation.

In June 1973 two White Papers were published. Whilst "Widening the Choice: the Next Steps" mainly focused on ideas for extending home ownership, it also contained a statement of the Government's view that a municipal monopoly of rented housing was unhealthy, and set out a policy commitment *"to expand the role of the voluntary housing sector as a provider of rented housing, and especially where the decline of the rented sector has created severe problems".*

The second White Paper "Better Homes: the Next Priorities" focused on policies for area-based regeneration, particularly powers enabling local authorities to declare Housing Action Areas (HAAs) in neighbourhoods of serious housing stress. The proposals reflected the evidence that the voluntary improvement focus of General Improvement Areas was not working in the worst stress areas, and that stronger powers of intervention were needed. The White Paper was explicit that *"the Government will look to housing associations increasingly to acquire and manage properties in HAAs".* The evidence from the Colville/Tavistock study area had been a significant influence on the thinking in the White Paper.

Interestingly, neither White Paper gave details of the new subsidy system for housing associations. Nor did they include proposals on the new role for the Housing Corporation in regulating housing associations and administering the new financial regime. All this could have been lost when the Conservative Government was defeated in the snap "Who governs Britain?" election called by prime minister Heath on February 28 1974. However, the incoming Labour Government re-introduced the Bill unchanged.

The new Secretary of State was Anthony Crosland. Formidably confident and iconoclastic, he had a reputation as one of Labour's leading intellectuals and policy thinkers. Having shadowed the Environment post, he had developed clear ideas on the housing strategy which a Labour Government should follow. By coincidence, he also lived on the slopes of Ladbroke Grove looking down on the streets where the Trust had long laboured.

Crosland had abandoned the traditional hostility felt by many people in the Labour Party to housing associations, and supported them being given a greatly enhanced role. His Second Reading speech on the Conservative Bill had also argued strongly the case for the use of compulsory purchase powers where this was needed to secure the improvement of sub-standard, privately rented property. It echoed more or less exactly the case the Trust had been advocating as essential for the improvement of the Colville/Tavistock area.

The new policies, both locally and nationally, gave the inner city "rehab" housing associations everything they could have hoped for. The new Act provided 100% capital grant to meet development deficits and higher management allowances for associations working in higher cost areas with vulnerable tenants. There were also stronger powers to secure improvements in areas of inner city housing stress.

The Act also contained a power for the Government to pay revenue deficit grant to meet unavoidable and unforeseen losses incurred by housing associations. This was similar to the financial agreement that Kensington and Chelsea Council had made with housing associations in 1970, but when the 1974 Housing Bill was published it did not include any such powers.

The clause proposing the power to give revenue deficit grant was tabled by Hugh Rossi MP, who was a former Conservative Housing Minister. Initially this was resisted by civil servants, who argued that the Treasury had made no financial provision for such payments. However, Ministers were persuaded to accept the amendment. Revenue Deficit Grant was to become a vital helpline for inner city housing associations, such as Notting Hill.

Lord Goodman, well-known as the Mr Fixit solicitor for the great and good who became the new Chairman of the Housing Corporation, was a close personal adviser to Harold Wilson, back in No 10 as Prime Minister. Goodman's · appointment was the clearest possible signal that the Corporation would carry real political clout. It did.

The fact was underlined by the appointments made to top officer posts at the Corporation. The new Chief Executive was Dick Madge and the Deputy Chief Executive was John Baker. As senior officials in the DoE they had played leading roles in framing the legislation and development of the new policies.

There was an extraordinary convergence of support for the new policies. It was one of those rare moments in post-war, British, public policy when leading politicians across the political spectrum, senior civil servants, and key voluntary sector agencies, all agreed and worked together to achieve the changes in legislation and policy they saw as necessary.

Looking back with the benefit of hindsight, it is easy to forget how many obstacles and uncertainties there were to the expansion of housing association activity at that time.

The Report of the Milner Holland Committee, the most comprehensive and authoritative examination of London's housing problems, had concluded that housing associations seemed unlikely to make a significant contribution to providing more affordable rented housing for low income families.

Even when the 1974 Housing Act became law, there were many people – including senior officials in Whitehall - who were doubtful about whether housing associations would expand on the scale required to make a significant difference.

The dramatic growth in the number of new homes provided by housing associations over the next few years showed that the sceptics had been wrong. It was a notable triumph for the new leadership of the National Federation of Housing Associations and the small group of housing associations who had lobbied so effectively.

Chapter 8

THE VOICE OF TENANTS

The small group of people who met in the Kenricks' house to found a new housing association had no idea they were setting up what would become a large, complex organisation, owning properties worth billions of pounds, employing over 700 staff and with an annual budget of £100 million.

In the early days, the staff were known personally to many of the tenants, and were visible in the Trust office or on the streets in the course of their daily work. Inevitably this situation changed as more properties were acquired, especially when more than half the houses were outside North Kensington and some distance from the Trust's office.

Initially the focus of the staff and committee was almost exclusively on the practical problems of buying, converting and letting homes. However, as the Trust grew and increasingly came to be seen as an important and powerful organisation, questions were asked about who made decisions and how they were made.

Was the Trust *"doing the Council's job"* and *"letting the Council off the hook?"* *"Who was the Trust housing?"*, *"Who was it accountable to?"* Some believed it was housing too many black people, others too few black people, but both believed the community should know. In the long campaign to change the Council's housing policies, the Peoples' Association saw the Trust as their most important ally in keeping homes for local residents. At the same time disgruntled black activists displayed the banner "Don't trust the Trust".

In response to these differing pressures the Trust began to evolve new arrangements for opening up access to its decision-making. John Coward was a strong believer in working with the local community and encouraging active participation by tenants. In a note written for this book he has described the thinking within the Trust:

"This pressure chimed with the very active dialogue in the voluntary housing sector on the subject of 'governance'. Issues of tenant participation and local accountability were very much to the fore in housing associations like ourselves working in other inner city areas. They were high on the agenda at every housing meeting and conference.

The problem faced was twofold. Firstly, how to define accountability in a relatively small local organisation like the Trust. Did this mean accountability to tenants or to the local community at large in a situation where operations were beginning to spread over quite a wide area of west London? Did this entitle those elected to represent the community?

Secondly, how to establish acceptable representation without losing momentum and cohesion and deflecting energy from what was a highly stressed operation, and without losing hitherto clear aims and uncomplicated decision making.

A step by step approach was adopted and the first step was to encourage the setting up of tenants' associations to represent the views of tenants. Then when an interested group began to form, to assist that group with duplicating facilities, lists of tenants in a particular area, postage costs etc and sometimes temporary use of premises that were empty and awaiting conversion.

The framework envisaged was that tenants' associations would then have their own procedures for electing or nominating representatives to serve on Trust committees. This system worked well. Several people served for a number of years and as 'members' were elected onto committees in their own right. They were knowledgeable and motivated individuals and as 'representatives' of a constituency they added great strength to the functioning of the committee generally".

Representation on the Area Committees and the Board has been one way in which the voice of tenants has been expressed in the Trust. Tenant participation has also been encouraged through support for tenants' associations and open meetings to discuss issues affecting particular groups. Where tenants have wanted to play a more active role in running their own homes, the Trust has supported the setting up of Tenant Management Co-operatives.

Two Area Committees were set up in 1974, one for North Kensington and the second for the Western Area. These were followed in 1981 by the setting up of an Area Committee in Earls Court, following the Trust's acquisition of properties there. The following year the Western Area was divided into two, with one Area Committee for Hammersmith and Fulham, and the other covering Ealing and Hounslow.

The Area Committees comprised members from the Trust's Committee of Management, including the chair of the Area Committee; members of local organisations; a local councillor; and two tenant representatives. According to John Coward the Area Committees were seen as both a way of responding to the pressure from the local community and opening up a door to the Committee of Management.

Shortly after the North Kensington Area Committee was set up Anthony Perry became the Chair, and played a significant part in developing its role. At the time he was the Director of the Motorway Development Trust, which was developing ambitious plans for the use of the land under the Westway flyover.

Another early member of that Committee, as well as being a member of the Committee of Management, was Rev Donald Eadie from the Methodist Group Ministry. He succeeded Rev Norwyn Denny, who had been a member of the Committee from the mid 1960s. Sue Black recalls the very active role some of the church groups played in the local community, in particular the very moving talk which Donald Eadie gave at the memorial service organised after a dreadful car accident in France when three members of the Trust staff were killed.

In 1976 Lionel Morrison was asked to become a member of the Committee of the Trust and also to join the newly created North Kensington Area Committee. Lionel had been born and grew up in South Africa. His family lived in one of the better townships on the edge of Johannesburg, but even there black families such as his experienced severe overcrowding. He became active politically in his teens, and was one of the youngest defendants in the Treason Trial in 1956. After serving 5 months in prison, including for his 21st birthday, he got a job as a journalist with the celebrated magazine, 'Drum'. Edited by Anthony Sampson, subsequently author of the 'Anatomy of Britain' series, Drum was then an isolated media voice critical of the apartheid regime.

In 1960 Lionel was advised to leave South Africa, because he was likely to be imprisoned again, and arrived as a stowaway at Southampton with £3.10s in his pocket. On reaching London he obtained work as a press officer with the Anti-Apartheid movement. Through family and friends in South Africa, he met Bruce Kenrick. As described in Chapter 8, he later became active in local organisations in Notting Hill, including in the black community, and was invited to become a member of the Trust's Committee.

As a young black journalist he applied for 170 jobs, with all kinds of publications, before eventually being offered a job by The People newspaper. At that time he was the only black journalist on Fleet Street. The paper was committed to covering social issues, and he was given an assignment to write a major feature on housing conditions in North Kensington and the controversial relationship between the black community and the police. This brought him to meet some of the best known members of the black community in the area, including Michael X, a flamboyant and controversial figure. He also met Frank Critchlow, who ran the Mangrove restaurant in All Saints Road.

During the early 70s Lionel Morrison was active with community groups in North Kensington, including the Golborne Project run by George Clark. In this period there was a feeling in the Trust of being under siege from critics in the local community.

At John Coward's request, Lionel invited Rhodan Gordon, a black activist who had been very critical of white organisations in the area, to become involved with the Trust. The recruitment of a well-known activist could be seen as an indication that the Trust was not taking the soft option of securing token black representation. It was Lionel's view that this enabled the Trust to become more confident in its relationships with local organisations. Lionel Morrison believes that the tenant representatives subsequently made a very valuable contribution to both the Area Committees and the Committee of Management. Some of the other members were surprised by the quality of such representatives. They had expected difficulties with tenants raising only their own grievances about issues such as repairs. Instead they found colleagues as eager as themselves to provide rounded and far-sighted judgements.

Tenant Representatives

The following section gives a description of a few of the tenant members who have served on the Area Committees, showing the range of experiences and qualities that they have brought.

The first tenant representative on the North Kensington Area Committee was Kay Dibley (later Zitron). She was joined shortly afterwards by Pat Macdonald. In 1979 they were elected as the first tenant members of the Committee of Management. Kay was a member for six years.

Kay Dibley had been given 6 months notice to leave a privately rented flat and was referred to the Trust by her health visitor because she was pregnant. She was housed by the Trust in a top floor, unconverted flat in Colville Square, but had a traumatic experience when the roof fell directly on top of her baby's cot. Fortunately, she had gone to stay with her mother for the weekend and the cot was empty.

As a result of this incident she was re-housed in a newly converted flat across the road in Colville Square. At the time, converted flats were being squatted as soon as the work was completed. The suspicion existed that information was being passed on by the decorators. Kay was offered the flat, and asked by the housing officer when she could move. Her reply was to start picking up the pram. She actually moved at 5.30 the same day.

She was encouraged to set up a tenants' association by her friend, Sue Porter. The first meeting took place in the premises of the Powis Playgroup. Kay became the secretary, and in 1976 the first tenant representative on the North Kensington Area Committee.

Initially she found some of the Area Committee members suspicious of her role, fearing, somewhat condescendingly, that she would only raise complaints about her own flat. Over time she found the tenant's contribution was welcomed. Soon she was invited to look at conversion plans with a housing officer and Sue Bird, the Kensington Development Manager. This process began because tenants often moved into new flats and said that the conversion would have been better executed if they had been consulted beforehand.

As time went by she got more and more calls from tenants, especially about repairs and allocations, and found her phone bill doubled. Having watched the work of the housing officers, she thought, "I can do this job", and successfully applied for a housing officer job with Paddington Churches Housing Association.

Pat Macdonald was a hugely energetic and formidable woman. She had been the first secretary of the Notting Hill People's Association, and was one of the local parents active in lobbying for the Colville Nursery Centre. By the mid-1970s she was an active participant in almost every area of community activity.

Sadly in 1986 she was murdered. A booklet "Pat Macdonald: Working Class Heroine" was published in her memory by friends and former colleagues to celebrate her life and the exceptional contribution she had made to the local community. She had lived and worked in North Kensington from the 1950s until her death. She was the driving force behind successful campaigns for better housing, more playspace and new nurseries.

Her special qualities were described in the booklet by Bill Richardson, a long time resident in North Kensington and friend of Pat's for many years:

"Pat was a gadfly, a catalyst, one who disturbs and shakes up, but for a purpose – to enable ordinary people to realise their own strength and creativity. Look around you at the nurseries and clubs for the young, houses now in the control of the trusts, safe from the rapacity of private landlords. Notting Hill now is a vastly different place from that of the 1950s. It all had to be fought for, it will not last unless the fight is kept up."

Mary Burke became a member of the Ealing and Hounslow Area Committee when it was first set up, and also a member of the Committee of Management. She was a tenant representative on the Board for over 15 years until 2004. She grew up in Ireland and came to London as a young woman to train as a nurse at the Royal Brompton Hospital in the southern end of Kensington and Chelsea. While there she married and had a baby, but her husband subsequently left her and she also lost her home. The hospital gave Mary accommodation in the Nurses Home, but she was unable to keep her baby there, who was taken temporarily into care.

Fortunately the Hospital was very sympathetic and requested help for housing from Kensington and Chelsea Council. It gave Mary a letter to the

Kensington Housing Trust asking if it could provide her with a flat. Armed with a letter to take to their offices, she was unfamiliar with the North Kensington area and lost her way. By chance she found the offices of the Notting Hill Housing Trust. While she was waiting to ask for directions, John Coward saw her and read the letter. Rather than simply refer Mary to KHT he decided to ask for the referral from the Council to be transferred to Notting Hill. He told Mary that she would hear from him shortly. Six weeks later she received an offer of a one bedroom flat in Cambridge Gardens.

This incident shows the direct and personal way the Trust could respond in the early days, albeit only for a small number of applicants. Having moved into North Kensington Mary was keen to be active in the local community. The Trust suggested ways in which she could help as a volunteer.

Whilst living in Cambridge Gardens she married again and had another baby. The flat was now too small and she was offered a transfer to a larger one in the Ealing area.

At this stage the Trust did not have many tenants in Ealing. The Trust properties were scattered over quite a wide area and no tenant associations had been set up there for Trust tenants. As a result it was decided to invite individual tenants to join the Area Committee.

Mary feels that *"the Trust empowered me. It helped me get back on my feet"*. As well as being on the Area Committee and a member of the Board for many years, she became active in the womens movement and with Acton Womens Aid.

Annabel Louvros was a member of the North Kensington Area Committee for 8 years until it was replaced by the Neighbourhood Board in 2002, and she then became a member of that.

She was born in Ladbroke Gardens in North Kensington, where her mother still lives as a private tenant. When Annabel grew up and married, she was unable to find a home that she could afford and spent four years on the Trust's waiting list, still living with her mother. When the Trust offered her a flat in All Saints Road, she found this difficult because of social problems in the area, but was given a transfer to a flat in Ladbroke Grove in 2000. She says that she feels passionate about living in North Kensington, and now has a flat which she loves:

"Every day as I put the key in my door, I thank God for this flat and being able to live in this area".

Over the years there has been considerable discussion about the role of the Area Committees in the Trust. A continuing tension has been between the pressures for more centralisation and for the retention of local management.

On the one side has been the wish to have a single central Board, which is able to make decisions quickly on issues such as approving new development projects. On the other side has been the desire for more devolution of responsibility, which enables tenant representatives and members from the local community to have a greater say.

By the early 1990s some people believed the Trust had become more centralised and that less importance was being given to the work of the Area Committees.

Amongst the findings of a Tenants Survey in 1993 were that 55% of tenants felt that *"the Trust could do a lot more to find out about tenants' views on housing"*. As a result the number of tenant representatives on the Area Committees was increased. The Trust held its first Tenant Conference and started to produce a separate Annual Report to Tenants, in addition to the Trust's overall Annual Reports.

The Customer Services Review in 2002 led to the decision to set up a central call centre and to close the Area offices. A functional management structure was created, with the Area Director posts being abolished. Initially, the Area Committees were retained, but without the local focus provided through the Area teams the committee members became frustrated by their ineffectiveness. As a result the Area Committees were replaced by Neighbourhood Boards.

However, there was strong criticism from tenant representatives that these new arrangements did not work satisfactorily. As a result it was decided to carry out a major review of tenant participation within the Trust. Consultants were appointed to arrange focus groups and random interviews were conducted with a sample of residents. There was positive feedback on the way the review was carried out.

Following this review, it was decided not to revive the Neighbourhood Boards, and to create more effective ways of promoting resident involvement. A new Housing Services Committee will have 4 tenant members. The new strategy for resident involvement aims to secure broad involvement of residents across the work of the Group. This includes agreeing a tenant compact, building on existing regeneration activities, ensuring black and ethnic minority residents and people with disabilities are involved, revitalising resident involvement at the local level and embedding resident involvement in the work of all staff so as "to make it the responsibility of everyone rather than the few".

Chapter 9

HIGH NOON OF RENEWAL

Following the passing of the 1974 Housing Act the Trust embarked on a huge programme of expansion to provide rented homes through acquiring and converting older houses. Recognising the importance of sustaining socially balanced communities the Trust also pioneered the development of shared ownership for those on middle incomes who were increasingly not able to obtain homes that they could afford in areas where housing was becoming expensive.

The Trust also extended its activities within the community, notably by supporting ground-breaking plans for a new Nursery Centre in North Kensington and by providing premises for local businesses in All Saints Road. Meanwhile the organisation continued to grow, making heavy demands on its able and committed staff, and stabilizing its financial position after many years of insecurity.

The Housing Act led to an immediate upsurge in housing association development. Initially there was no limit to the number of approvals the Housing Corporation could give, as the Government's aim was to encourage associations to expand as rapidly as they could. In 1975 approvals were given for over 50,000 homes, an extraordinary rate of expansion. It reflected both the enthusiasm of housing associations to take advantage of the new opportunities, as well as the Government's support for a huge increase in Housing Corporation funding.

In addition to 100% loans and Housing Association Grant (HAG) subsidies, associations received an administrative allowance to meet the costs of negotiating purchases and preparing schemes. A Revenue Deficit Grant was also payable annually in arrears.

Not surprisingly when spending escalated so quickly, the Government soon felt it necessary to set limits for annual approvals, although at a very high level in comparison to previous levels of housing activity. The limits became stricter following the financial crisis which engulfed Britain in 1976 and the public spending cuts imposed on the Callaghan cabinet as a condition for an IMF loan. However, the Corporation's programme was maintained at a high level throughout the 1970s. This period was the housing association movement's golden age.

In 1974 the Trust owned 819 properties, which would provide almost 2,400 homes when all the properties were converted. By 1979 the number had more than doubled to 4,841. This was made up of 3,200 homes fully converted, 827 still unconverted and 814 under building contract.

Work in Kensington and Chelsea

The Council's Colville/Tavistock Housing Action Area (HAA) was declared in December 1974, becoming the first in the country. It was followed a few months later by a second HAA and together they covered the whole of the area covered by the Colville/Tavistock study.

When the first HAA was declared there were 1051 households living there, occupying 387 properties. Of these 193 were considered satisfactory, 129 houses in multiple occupation and 44 single-family houses were deemed unsatisfactory, almost all of them owned by private landlords. By the end of the HAA's life five years later, virtually all of the unsatisfactory properties had been improved or were in the process of being improved.

In 1979 the Trust published the results of a study carried out by John Palmer, a researcher who had been one of the authors of the report of the 1967 Housing Survey carried out by the Summer Project. The report "A Decade of New Housing in Notting Hill", examined the results of the public housing programme carried out in North Kensington between 1968 and 1978.

The study included a map showing the distribution of the properties owned by the Trust across North Kensington. It showed that two thirds were in the W11 postal district, especially in the Colville/Tavistock Housing Action Areas. However, the Trust also owned street properties across a wide area of North Kensington.

During this period the Kensington Housing Trust was also carrying out a major programme, mainly through redevelopment in the Golborne ward, lying immediately north of the Colville area. The GLC was responsible for the redevelopment of the Swinbrook area, also in the Golborne ward. The choice of clearance and new development, rather than rehabilitation, had been made by the Council on account of the poorer physical condition of the properties in the Golborne area.

The study made an assessment of the combined effects of the activity by housing associations, the Borough Council and the GLC. In 1971 there were a total of 23,250 dwellings in North Kensington. By 1982 7,450 new or improved homes would be provided, two thirds by housing associations, a quarter by the Borough Council and 10% by the GLC.

Within a short period a huge change in housing conditions across North Kensington had been achieved as a result of action by social housing agencies, with Notting Hill and Kensington Housing Trusts playing the major roles. By the end of the 1970s there were very few remaining of the decaying, multi-occupied properties which had so shocked Bruce Kenrick when he arrived in Notting Hill in 1962. There was still work to be done, but the transformation was remarkable.

Developing in Hammersmith and Fulham

During the 1960s the Trust had started to acquire properties outside North Kensington because they were cheaper and easier to purchase. Most of these were in Hammersmith and Fulham, but also in Ealing and Hounslow. Properties in these boroughs were known as being in the Western Area.

As a result of these purchases, in 1974, the number of units was slightly greater in the Western Area (1193) than in North Kensington (1158). Initially all the houses in the Western Area were used to re-house people from North Kensington, using loans from the Greater London Council or Kensington and Chelsea Council. The Trust did not have any direct agreements with any of the three boroughs.

Most of the properties outside North Kensington were in Hammersmith and Fulham, where the Trust owned 913 units. These were mainly concentrated in the north of the borough, especially in Shepherd's Bush, which was the area adjoining North Kensington, albeit divided by the north-south spur of the ill-fated inner London motorway box which ended abruptly (and forever) at the Shepherd's Bush roundabout. To the north and west of the roundabout the area contained a large number of old terraced street properties, owned by private landlords, which the Trust was able to purchase.

The Trust's policy of using the properties bought in the Western Area to re-house tenants from North Kensington inevitably meant that they were not available to help people with housing problems living in those areas. One person who became concerned by this was Rev John Ashbridge, the Vicar of St Stephens and St Thomas's Church in Shepherd's Bush. He had taken over responsibility for the parish in 1966, and soon found that families were coming to the door of the vicarage asking for help with their desperate housing problems.

"Offering them prayers did not seem enough", he said and decided to set up a housing association to help them. Rather than competing with the Notting Hill Housing Trust in buying properties in the Shepherd's Bush area he went to see John Coward to ask if some of the houses being bought by the Trust in Shepherd's Bush could be let to those families. John agreed to propose that the Trust would offer nominations rights to some of these properties. However, when this was put to the Committee of the Trust, they

turned it down. *"Bugger this"*, was John Ashbridge's response: *"We'll do it ourselves, and we did"*.

Although its scale of activities was much smaller than Notting Hill's, the Shepherd's Bush Housing Association succeeded in buying properties in Hammersmith and Fulham, and later expanded to other boroughs in west London. Initially John Ashbridge combined running the association with his duties as a vicar, but as the work expanded he secured the agreement of his bishop to work full-time as Director of the Association. He continued in that role until he retired in 1989.

One of the curates at the church was a young, black clergyman, Rev Wilfred Wood. He was very actively involved in race relations work, both locally and nationally, including as Chair of the British Council of Churches Race Relations Committee. Within the parish he saw the effects on black families of living in poor housing, and actively supported the setting up of the new housing association. He was a member of the committee until his appointment as Bishop of Croydon, becoming the first black bishop in Britain.

The Notting Hill Housing Trust's practice of buying houses outside North Kensington was also causing concern to the local authority in Hammersmith and Fulham, as the borough had significant housing needs itself.

The Labour-controlled Council elected in 1971 was initially hostile to housing associations. Its members believed that only the local authority should be providing rented housing. However, a small group of councillors wanted the Notting Hill Housing Trust to be active in their borough too. They saw this as especially important because the Council's redevelopment programme was coming to an end, and the next priority was the renovation of older housing. Housing associations were particularly well fitted for this role.

These members arranged an initial informal meeting with John Coward. Unusually for him, he had not written his speech in advance, but captivated his listeners with a spell-binding presentation.

The meeting with councillors was followed by a meeting with the Director of Housing, Derek Fox, and Tony Babbage, who was the Assistant Director responsible for housing improvements in the private sector in the Environmental Health Department. Both these officers also wanted to expand the work of housing associations in the Borough and to ensure that new homes were offered to applicants on the Council's own waiting list.

As a result of the discussions with the Trust, the Council reversed its previous policy of not supporting housing associations. In 1973 agreement was reached with the Trust for a sizeable annual programme of acquisitions and conversions. This included the arrangement with the GLC that where they made loans to the Trust new lettings would be shared on an equal basis between nominees from Hammersmith and Fulham and those from Kensington and Chelsea, rather than given solely to those nominated from Kensington and Chelsea as had happened previously.

The north Hammersmith area contained a particularly large number of Victorian street properties, most of them smaller than the houses in North Kensington. The area had not experienced to the same extent the problems caused by Rachman and similar rogue landlords. However, there were serious problems of housing stress, including neighbourhoods with high concentrations of sub-standard properties, overcrowding, and shared facilities. Roger Tuson, who was the Deputy Director of the Trust in the late 1970s, recalls that he saw worse conditions of overcrowding and disrepair in some of those houses than he has seen anywhere else.

A Huge Programme of Housing Action Areas
Hammersmith and Fulham Council decided that many of these areas were suited for the new Housing Action Area (HAA) powers and embarked on a major programme of declaring such areas. In total the Borough declared 18 Housing Action Areas. The total number of HAAs declared by over 350 housing authorities in England and Wales between 1974 and 1979 was only 449, so the programme in Hammersmith and Fulham was one of the largest in the country.

Each HAA had a nominated housing association to buy and renovate properties. The Notting Hill Housing Trust was asked to work in ten of them and Shepherd's Bush Housing Association in the other eight. In each area the Council opened a local office and appointed a small team to co-ordinate the work. For the smaller HAAs the Project teams covered more than one Area.

A detailed survey was carried out before the declaration of each Area, which identified ownership of all the houses and reported on those which were not in a satisfactory condition. Following inspections, notices were served on the owners setting out the work required to meet the necessary standard. They were also informed of the improvement grants available as well as the option of selling to a housing association if owners were unwilling to carry out the improvements themselves.

If the necessary work was not carried out, a formal notice was served requiring it to be done. If the landlord failed to respond to this notice the Council could use its powers to serve a Compulsory Purchase Order (CPO). The Council made regular use of these powers where they had evidence that the properties were in poor condition and the owner showed no signs of carrying out improvements.

In each instance a formal resolution was brought to the Housing Committee and the full Council to seek authorisation for the use of these

Early 1960s advertisement in The Guardian.

Years of neglect turned properties into slums.

People tried to keep clean and tidy in the grimmest of conditions.

The Reverend Bruce Kenrick,
founder of Notting Hill Housing Trust.

John Coward OBE,
Director until 1986.

Anthony Taussig, committee member
1968-2004 and chair 1988-1994.

Pansey Jeffrey, early
committee member.

*Sidney Miller of Family Service Unit,
early committee member.*

*Sir Roger Ormrod, chair 1968-1988 with
HRH The Duchess of Gloucester, Patron.*

*Furniture van operated by volunteers delivering
to the Trust's first charity shop 1970s.*

Staff and volunteers in the 1970s.

Landlords illegally trying to clear tenants out of properties,
stopped carrying out repairs.

Family of six living in one room.

New home in 1970s.

Colville Square during works.

VIII

*Tavistock Road, Royal Borough of Kensington
and Chelsea, before works were carried out.*

Norland Square, London Borough of Hammersmith and Fulham, before works.

Norland Square, after works completed.

All Saints Road shops after renovation with Urban Development Grant.

Trillington House, Uxbridge Road, Shepherd's Bush,
first sheltered housing scheme.

Kids at fun day consultation event on one of the new estates.

Ruby Wax helps in the Lime Grove homeless hostel fundraising in 1990s.

Rootes factory site housing development.

Salamanca Place, London Borough of Lambeth -
shared ownership homes for key workers. (photo credit: Nic Miller)

Isokon Building, London Borough of Camden - shared ownership homes for key workers. (photo credit: Emma Croxall)

Shaftesbury Place homes over Tescos - shared ownership homes.

John Coward in 2004 at the opening of the new baby room at the Colville Nursery Centre, which he helped set up in 1974 when heading up the Trust.

powers. Each CPO needed approval by the Secretary of State, following a public inquiry. Where it was approved, the property was transferred to the ownership of a housing association. Frequently the threat of a CPO persuaded the owner to sell the property to a housing association, which then re-housed the tenants and converted the property into self-contained flats.

The first Housing Action Area was declared in September 1975 in the Coningham Road area, situated to the west of Shepherd's Bush Green in the northern part of the borough. Fortunately for the Trust their Western Area offices were in Coningham Road itself and therefore it was ideally placed to be the lead association, with a local presence in the area.

The report produced at the end of the 5 year life of the HAA showed that improvements had been completed on 522 homes, with work in progress on another 175. By the end of the programme a total of 700 improved homes would be provided. The Trust had completed improvements to provide 140 self-contained dwellings.

David Barlow worked as the Project leader for the Coningham Road HAA and three other smaller areas. After graduating he had lived in Guildford, working as a scientist, and became active with the local Shelter group, running a small housing advice centre and campaigning to secure better provision for homeless people. As a result of this experience, he abandoned his scientific career in order to obtain a full-time job in housing with Hammersmith and Fulham Council. After an initial training period he was appointed to his post with the Housing Action Areas, and after five years moved in 1982 to become the development manager for the Trust in the western area.

He believes that the Housing Action Areas were responsible for significant improvements in housing conditions, especially the multi-occupied properties owned by the private landlords who were *"making a good living running grotty flats"*.

He recalls that some landlords reacted aggressively, and even violently, to demands to improve their properties. On one occasion the landlord came into the Trust office in Coningham Road and threatened to attack the member of staff who was there. In another incident a staff member was chased out of a house by the landlord holding a gun.

Sue Ellenby worked as a housing officer in the Trust's Coningham Road office. It was her first job in housing, after working for three years in a citizens advice bureau and a short period as a housing trainee with Hammersmith and Fulham Council. She later became the Director of the London Housing Federation between 1997 and 2004.

She says that she loved her work with the Trust, especially working so close to where tenants were living. One of her tasks was to arrange re-housing for the sitting tenants in properties bought by the Trust. While many were desperate to move, some older tenants were reluctant to leave despite the archaic conditions they lived in. Sue remembers one old lady who lived in a dark basement flat with an outside WC, who absolutely refused to move. Eventually the Trust gave up trying to persuade her that she might be better off in a newly modernized flat and renovated the rest of the house. She stayed in her flat whilst the rest of the property was converted – an early example of "tenants choice".

Several of the reports produced by the Council at the end of the HAA's life highlighted the importance of the Trust's role.

In the Devonport Road HAA the Council report said:

"The Notting Hill Housing Trust has successfully acquired 43 properties since the HAA declaration. Of these 32 have been improved to provide 97 dwellings. Works are in progress on 10 properties and a further 4 properties are in the programme for works to start shortly. Clearly the work by the Trust has been crucial to the successful implementation of the HAA programme".

In the College Park HAA the Council report in April 1982 concluded:

"The work of the Notting Hill Housing Trust has been crucial in the successful implementation of the Housing Action Area programme. 73 dwellings have been provided, with over 95% of these being offered to local College Park residents".

Several of the Council reports highlighted the value of the Trust's work in improving the worst properties in the Areas. For example, in both the Baron's Court and the Strode Road Areas the Council stressed that:

"Although the Trust has not acquired a large number of properties, its contribution had been valuable by virtue of selectively purchasing and improving some of the worst properties. It has helped lift the neighbourhood".

In the Sherbroke Road HAA the Council report in November 1983 stressed both the value of the Trust's work in improving poor properties, and also the positive feedback on the quality of the work and the success in re-housing local residents:

"Notting Hill have played a very valuable role in improving many of the tenanted dwellings for fair renting, most of which were the worst in terms of repair and amenities in the area. At the recent Open Day, Members will recall the high standard of improvements to the flats and the fact that it had been possible to retain most of the tenants who previously lived in the road".

A report to the Council's Housing Committee in October 1983 summarized the progress achieved in the HAAs over the previous seven years:

"Since the programme began over 2,000 homes have been improved in HAAs. Of these 25% have been improved by the Council, 30% by the partner housing associations and 45% by the private sector".

One of the important achievements of the HAA programme was that it did not rely solely on publicly funded work, but led to considerable investment by private owners. The detailed reports demonstrate visible results in a range of ways:

- Improvements carried out by private owners, many with the help of grants.
- Properties bought and improved by the Council and housing associations.
- Re-housing of local residents, so that they could remain in the same area.

These contrast with the criticisms of what had happened in areas needing improvements prior to the Housing Action Area provisions of the 1974 Housing Act. A succession of reports on local areas had consistently criticised the lack of activity by private landlords, and the displacement of low income tenants when properties were bought and improved by private owners, usually middle class incomers "colonising" new areas for gentrification.

The HAA programme in Hammersmith and Fulham achieved outstanding results, and the Notting Hill Housing Trust was a leading partner in ten of the Areas. Perhaps surprisingly none of its Annual Reports of the period highlight such results, and it has not been highlighted as one of the Trust's important achievements.

Pat White, who was responsible for the Trust's media and publicity recalls the lack of press interest in what was being done. Compared to North Kensington *"there were no rows"*. Journalists were not interested. There had been no Rachmans, no ethnic conflict, no carnival to stimulate the febrile collective imagination of the metropolitan media – many of whom actually lived locally, part of the gentrification which was inevitable when potentially desirable streets were so close to the BBC Television Centre in Wood Lane.

The Council itself did record the progress achieved in the HAAs. However by the early 1980s, it was more concerned to secure improvements in the areas which had not been covered by the programme. They developed proposals for creating "Housing Improvement Zones", to cover the properties outside existing HAAs. Although these did not contain such intensive problems of multi-occupation and poor conditions, substantial numbers of the properties needed improvement.

However, the Zones did not have any extra statutory powers or attract additional resources. By the early 1980s local authority capital resources were being reduced by central government. The national housing agenda was dominated by debates about the Right to Buy policy. Housing renewal, especially in areas of housing stress, was no longer a political priority.

Low cost home ownership

In 1976 the Trust started to look at the possibilities for offering low cost home ownership to local people who were not able to afford the full cost of buying their home. It set up a working party to examine what it called "Middle Range" housing.

The awareness of this need grew partly from the experience of working intensively with the residents in the Colville/Tavistock area, and seeing the danger that the community could become polarised between affluent home owners and low income tenants.

The Trust's lettings in the area were almost all going to people on low incomes, who had been tenants in the properties when they were bought, or to applicants nominated by the Council. The privately owned housing was becoming expensive and out of reach of people on middling incomes.

The Trust had been formed to respond to the desperate needs of families who were being made homeless or living in severely overcrowded accommodation. As it grew to become a leading provider of good quality rented homes in the area, John Coward saw that there was also a need to provide homes for those who were not a priority for socially rented housing, but could not afford outright home ownership. As he saw the housing market in North Kensington *"the middle range was missing"*.

The task of investigating new options was given to Andrew Williamson, who had recently joined the Trust from working with Richard Best at the British Churches Housing Trust. Over the next three years Andrew worked at developing a new model of part-owned, part-rented housing. The applicants would buy 50% of the property by taking on a mortgage, and the housing association would buy the other 50%. The Housing Corporation would pay Housing Association Grant on the costs of buying and converting this half of the property, so as to reduce the level of rent payable. Like other Trust innovations the concept would later find far wider application.

As there were no precedents, developing the model required an enormous amount of work. This included investigating the financial implications on a range of different property values, developing a lease which reflected the rights and responsibilities of the different parties, and discussions with the local authority, private lenders and government officials – and crucially exploring what the demand might be from potential customers.

A lot of discussions were held with Rosie Boughton at the National Federation of Housing Associations, who was also investigating the feasibility of what was being known as "community leasehold", in order to distinguish it from the traditional image of home ownership and stress its links to socially owned rented housing. The Trust also had productive discussions with officials in the Department of the Environment, who were keen to encourage housing associations to provide an alternative to rented accommodation which needed less subsidy.

Notting Hill was the first association to research community leasehold and turn it into new homes, although a few others followed the example shortly afterwards. There was a vigorous debate internally in the Trust about whether it should be promoting shared ownership at all. Some saw it as a diversion from the task of providing rented homes for people on low incomes, especially where the unmet need was still so great. There was a concern that money spent on new shared ownership schemes would be taken from the budget for rented housing.

Initially, however, the scale of plans for this new form of housing tenure was small. The first scheme to be completed was at 88 Ladbroke Grove in North Kensington. Reg Freeson, the Labour Minister of Housing, was invited to open the scheme, but the 1979 General Election took place before the opening. John Stanley, Freeson's successor, agreed to open it instead. It was one of his first official engagements.

Working with the local community:

Regeneration of All Saints Road
One road in North Kensington was increasingly of special concern for the Trust. All Saints Road was right in the heart of the Trust's activities. It was located to the east of Portobello Road, south of the Hammersmith and City branch of the London Underground, and north of Westbourne Park Road, which separated it from Colville and Powis Squares. The properties were mostly four and five storey, terraced houses, with mixed use comprising a shop on the ground floor and basement and residential accommodation on the floors above.

Close to the junction of All Saints Road with Westbourne Park Road was the Mangrove restaurant, owned and run by Frank Critchlow. Since the late 1960s it had been a well-known meeting place for members of the Caribbean community from across London and those visiting from other parts of the country and overseas, among them musicians, writers and political activists. The street corner outside was also a popular gathering point for young West Indians, who liked and respected Frank Critchlow, an older black leader willing to give them advice and support.

The Mangrove was thus a very popular meeting place, both for many black activists and white progressives, but Frank Critchlow only rented the building. One well-known figure in the black community was Lionel Morrison. He drew together a small group who devised a scheme to buy the property. They persuaded a hundred people to lend a minimum of £100 for ten years, and this raised enough to buy the Mangrove building for £6,500, leaving the balance for repairs that might be needed. Each year ten people, drawn by lot, received their money back from the profits of the restaurant.

All Saints Road was also where the Trust's new offices had been built. So tenants were regularly coming to report repairs or discuss rent payments alongside others enquiring about possibilities of re-housing. Staff of the Trust were also frequently walking up or down the Road.

However, as the Trust's activities improved the surrounding streets, All Saints Road stood in stark contrast. It remained almost the only street which showed the physical decay which had been so prevalent in the area in the Rachman era. This was shown at its worst by the derelict commercial properties, with empty flats above. They symbolized the economic decline of a run-down inner city area. Instead of being home to local shops and businesses their only use was for drug dealing and illegal drinking shabeens.

After much discussion the Trust decided that the key to the regeneration of the street was to bring the commercial properties into responsible ownership. As a result, the first mixed use portfolio was acquired in 1972. The local authority responded positively to the Trust's plans and actively assisted in trying to achieve improvements in the street.

Behind this innovation lay a further important goal. Above the shops were usually flats, equally neglected. Very often they were recognisable by a cracked beam – a Bessamer beam – holding up the first floor. No one had the money or legal right to fix it. The problem was simple. It was hard to obtain a conventional mortgage covering a domestic residential property and a commercial property. Yet both shops and the flats above them were in desperately short supply. By devising a funding mechanism which got round this problem the Trust had unlocked a valuable social asset in communities that most needed them.

It was decided that it was very important that the new shops and business premises created should be used by the local community, and especially that opportunities be open to local black businesses. Funding was raised for a Small Business Adviser to advise new companies setting up.

Pat White, who was responsible for managing the project, recalls walking up and down the road collecting rents from the new businesses. No money was ever stolen. In the late 1970s when there were violent confrontations at the Notting Hill Carnival and shop windows smashed in many streets in the area, the businesses in All Saints Road were untouched. So it proved again during the widespread inner city urban riots in Brixton, Liverpool and elsewhere in 1981.

In 1980, the Trust set up NHHT Commercial Properties Ltd to manage non-residential properties. The Department of the Environment had been concerned that in the activities of the Trust with non-residential properties, public money was being used to fund commercial activities. Setting up a separate subsidiary was a way of visibly demonstrating that this was not happening.

There had also been a lengthy debate with lawyers on whether letting commercial properties was a legitimate operation for a charitable housing association. Whilst it was eventually agreed this could be done legally it was a very unusual initiative for a housing association and fraught with risks. The operation could lose money if the shops failed to overcome the bad reputation of the street. The Trust could attract bad publicity if it was seen to be the landlord of properties where disreputable, even criminal activities were taking place.

During the next few years funding was obtained from the new Urban Development Grant fund to improve the shopfronts. In an unusual purchase, one of the two pubs in All Saints Road, the Apollo, was bought by NHHT Commercial Properties Ltd and converted into workshops.

The Colville Nursery Centre

Another important initiative in the early 1970s was the work to provide premises and raise funds for the Colville Nursery Centre. The Trust actively supported the development of a unique under 5s facility, which combined nursery education and day care within a fully integrated service.

The Centre's origins arose from the concern of local mothers using the Powis Playgroup, who wanted to see greater day care and nursery provision. They were also concerned by the very poor quality of child-minding experienced by a lot of young children.

The only alternative to private child-minders for mothers who worked full-time on low wages was council day care with no education element. The only education for under 5s in schools was limited to three hours a day in a nursery class, and it was often difficult for working mothers to take advantage of this.

At the time the Powis Playgroup was a member of the Westway Nursery Association which was seeking to promote better provision for young children in North Kensington, especially children of working mothers. Their vision was for something quite new in the world of day nurseries and nursery school provision: to integrate nursery day care and education within one centre.

The Nursery Centre would be free to all those using it, cater for the whole range of under 5 year old children, and be open for the full range of hours when mothers were working during the day. It would also be open through the school holidays, when working mothers needed provision for their children. The aim was that the nursery school provision would be funded by the Inner London Education Authority and the day nursery provision by the Borough Council Social Services.

The group approached John Coward to ask if a property could be made available, and the Trust would support the plans for setting up and financing a Nursery Centre. Initially the aim that the nursery should be free to the families using it seemed impossibly ambitious to the Trust, but the group was determined to achieve this.

Although there were nurseries in other parts of North Kensington there was no provision in the Colville/Powis area where the Trust's growing housing stock was most concentrated. So the Trust agreed to make available the basement and ground floor of three large houses it owned at 3/4/5 Colville Square, and to assist the Nursery Centre group in obtaining funding. Hunter and Partners, who handled a large part of the Trust's development programme, agreed to oversee the extensive conversion work free of charge.

Despite this important step forward, the practical and financial hurdles to be overcome in establishing the Nursery Centre remained daunting. They included setting up premises for a 50 place nursery, on terms which complied with demanding statutory requirements; and securing funding for the running costs over future years, including salaries for professional and support staff.

John Coward was asked to chair the Committee set up to plan the nursery, and played a key role in negotiations for funding from the two local authority bodies and in approaches to charitable trusts. He stayed as the Chair throughout the development period and the first three years of the Nursery's operation.

The negotiations to secure funding were long and complex, as there was no precedent for such a combined nursery service. To achieve success it was necessary to secure the support both of the Inner London Education Authority (ILEA), which had statutory responsibility for nursery education, and Kensington and Chelsea Borough Council, which had responsibility for day care for under 5's. This was far from easy as relations between ILEA and the Borough Council had been difficult. Fortunately, senior officers in both bodies proved very supportive. One important ally was Tina Broomberg, a black South African, who was the head of the Colville Primary School.

John Coward recalls the considerable expertise and determination of the group of women seeking to set up the Centre, which included Pat Macdonald, Jan O'Malley and Judy Wilcox, who later became the Co-ordinator of the Maxila Nursery Centre under the Westway flyover.

The person appointed as the Co-ordinator was Jenny Williams, who had been the Chair of the Westway Nursery Association. She had grown up in an Octavia Hill Housing Trust property in Notting Dale, where her mother had been the community nurse. She was a tireless activist in local community organisations, as well as being a long-standing member of the local Communist Party and an editorial member of the Morning Star.

John Coward believes the work with the Nursery Centre marked a turning point for the Trust, where it was able to broaden its role from only providing housing to becoming an agency supporting other organisations concerned with the wider social health of a deprived community. Looking back he feels that this project gave him *"the greatest satisfaction when remembering my time in Notting Hill"*.

When the Centre opened it soon became widely known, and was a frequent venue for visits by groups wanting to set up similar nursery centres elsewhere, as well as educational and social service professionals and visiting dignitaries.

The eclectic nature of the area could lead to misunderstandings. On one occasion, shortly before a planned visit by the Duke of Edinburgh, two smartly dressed men in suits appeared outside the Nursery Centre, looking up and down the street. Jenny Williams wrongly assumed that they were clients of "Big Lil", the well-known prostitute who lived in the basement of the house adjoining the Centre. Jenny pointed them downstairs. When the "suits" re-appeared a few moments later and disclosed their identity as members of the royal household there was embarrassment all round, though the story might well have amused the Duke.

"Big Lil" became a firm supporter of the Nursery Centre, and would often appear in the mornings with gifts such as expensive boxes of chocolates, presumably brought by one of her clients the night before. Such was another small aspect of the politics of wealth redistribution in a deprived neighbourhood.

Developing the organisation:

The North Kensington area

Nick Hughes joined the Trust in 1973 and shortly after became the Area Manager in North Kensington. After leaving university he had joined the civil service in the Ministry of Housing and Local Government. He joined on the same day as David Edmonds and Anthony Mayer, both of whom went on to become Chief Executives of the Housing Corporation. Nick, however, hated working in the civil service and left to join the Trust. In doing so he took a salary cut from £4,000 to £2,000. a lot of money at a time when a pound was worth at least ten times what it was by the end of the century.

Like many other new staff Nick had no previous experience of housing work. He describes his job as *"basically a manager of chaos"*. Shortly after he arrived there was an *"arrears explosion"*, and an enormous effort was needed to ensure that rents were paid regularly. At that time almost any vacant property was at risk of being squatted. Recovering possession was time-consuming and often difficult.

"In my first week I was in my office at Coningham Road and a large West Indian lady came in, very angry. I'd never met her before, but the discussion became very heated and she picked up a very large ashtray and hurled it at me. It made quite a big hole in the partition behind me".

Despite all this he relished the challenge. *"It transformed my life. For me personally it was wonderful, therapeutic. What made it great was the people".*

Sue Bird (later Black) joined the Trust in 1974. After a three-hour interview she was appointed to the post of Contract Liaison officer in the Development section. She went on to hold numerous posts in the organisation and was a member of the senior management team for over twenty years. Her jobs included being an Area Manager, Manager of Commercial Properties, Director of Home Ownership, Director of Operations and Deputy Chief Executive.

When she came to the Trust Sue had been working for a property developer. Like many refugees from local government or the private sector, most of them in search of more challenging work, she found the Trust very different. *"Everything was done in a really old-fashioned way, and I couldn't believe the conditions we worked in".* When she arrived there were few procedures in place. The priority had been buying more properties as fast as possible.

Adrian Maynard, the Trust's street-smart property buyer, had built up an extremely good knowledge of the local housing market, and was a key figure in the expansion of the Trust's development programme. Sue Black remembers Adrian, who died some years ago, as an *"ace negotiator for the Trust".*

She describes the process following one-off purchases of street properties as *"a game of chess".* Sitting tenants had to be rehoused to keep the development programme rolling, whilst the housing management staff were desperate to help families in acute housing need from the waiting list. There were tensions between different sections where delays in one stage caused problems in the next. Sue recalls *"there were some real rows, but over time good relationships were developed between the property and housing management teams".*

The Council surveyors were inspecting every property bought by the Trust in great detail, and cutting out any item of improvement they considered inessential. Pressure was relentless to get properties improved and occupied as quickly as possible, although later experience showed that problems caused by cost-savings could themselves be costly.

As the Trust grew rapidly, concern grew that the rate at which properties were being converted was not keeping pace with the rate of purchases. The result was a growing number of tenants living in unimproved homes. The problem was especially acute in North Kensington where more properties had been bought with sitting tenants.

One unusual volunteer working in the North Kensington office was Ralph Raby. He was a retired stockbroker, well-off and worldly in the ways of the City, who came in to the Trust every day in the late 1970s. He performed invaluable work speeding up the development programme, especially in reducing the number of properties waiting for conversion.

In Nick Hughes' view he was *"an unsung hero"*. Later he became a member of the Committee of Management of the Trust, and subsequently a committee member of the Catalyst Group, formerly the Ealing Family Housing Association.

The Western Area

During the 1970s the Western Area strengthened its distinctive identity. In Hammersmith and Fulham the Trust became the lead housing association working in the northern parts of the Borough. Shepherd's Bush Housing Association worked primarily in the southern area, but was less proactive in seeking new opportunities.

Edie Szep came to the Trust as a Housing Assistant in 1975 and stayed fifteen years. During that time she held six different jobs, ending up as the Area Director for Ealing, Hounslow and Hillingdon. She recalls:

"In the early days we were just winging it. People let you do whatever seemed sensible if it would help. I think the Trust chose staff not for their technical skills, but maybe because they spotted something else, that they thought people would be able to cope.

"Some tenants found it difficult to cope, including some who got into problems with their neighbours, and some who got into arrears with their rent. You tried to do everything you could to help tenants keep their homes and manage day to day. Eviction was the last resort. I wouldn't even say the last resort. It was never anything other than a form of a threat to get them to change their behaviour."

In 1979 it was decided to appoint Area Directors and devolve more responsibilities. Up until then, the Areas were responsible for housing management, but property purchasing, the development programme and housing maintenance were all run centrally. Under the new arrangements all development work was transferred to the Areas.

At that time Adrian Norridge was working as the Principal Homelessness and Lettings officer for Kensington and Chelsea Council, having decided to leave his teaching job. He had been a Labour councillor in Hammersmith and Fulham since 1971, and was one of the councillors who had invited John Coward to the meeting which led to the Trust being asked to work in the Borough.

Adrian had stood down as a councillor in 1979 and was keen to work for a housing association, but felt he would not yet be considered for a post at the Area Director level with Notting Hill. So he applied for and accepted a job with the Kensington Housing Trust.

He was taken aback when his wife - while enjoying a quiet bath one evening - took a phone call from John Coward wanting to speak urgently to him. When they spoke Adrian learnt that the Trust had not felt able to appoint a new Area Director from the candidates they had seen, and wanted urgently to discuss the post with him. Adrian explained that he had just accepted the Kensington Housing Trust offer, but asked if he could be interviewed in the next few days.

As a result it was arranged to meet early two days later, with a hastily assembled interview panel. Despite starting the interview by spilling his coffee over John Coward, Adrian was offered the post and withdrew his acceptance of the job at KHT.

When he started at the Western Area office Adrian was surprised by the lack of files. It appeared that with the rapid growth in acquiring and converting properties, the work of building up comprehensive records had not been carried out. One of his first tasks was to set up new administrative systems.

Over the next few years the Trust expanded its activities to work in the Borough of Ealing, where both members and officers supported the growth of housing association work. Prior to this time the properties bought in Ealing had been used to re-house tenants from properties bought in North Kensington. There had been no separate programme for work with the Council to assist their housing programme. During the 1980s the Trust became a partner with the Council, especially in buying and converting unmodernized, older street properties.

Between 1979 and 1986 the number of homes owned by the Trust in the Western Area more than doubled, from 1,900 to 4,800. When Adrian Norridge left in 1986 to become Chief Executive of St Pancras

Housing Association, it was decided to divide the area into two. Hammersmith and Fulham became one, with the second covering Ealing, Hounslow and Hillingdon, where the Trust wanted to become more active.

Achieving financial stability

Whilst the 1974 Act's system of Housing Association Grant had created an extremely favourable framework for future housing development, the Trust was incurring a deficit because of management and repair costs exceeding the revenue from rental income, especially since rent increases were limited by the 1972 Housing Finance Act to those approved by the independent Rent Officer.

These were the problems for which the provision for payment of Revenue Deficit Grant had been devised in the 1974 Act. The Trust was one of the first associations to seek help from this, and submitted a large claim for £498,569 for the financial year which ended September 1974.

However, each claim required detailed scrutiny by officials in the Department of the Environment. Although grants were discretionary, and had no fixed ceiling, the Department wanted to be satisfied that every penny of the claim had properly been spent on housing management and repairs work to the association's property. As the scheme was wholly new, there were no officials with previous experience of administering it.

As a result of these factors only £288,728 had been paid, all on account, by the time the second annual claim was due for the year ended September 1975. A similar lengthy process delayed settlement for the year ended September 1976. Although several payments on account were made, the total amount of the claims outstanding continued to rise.

The Trust's bank account was continually running at a level far in excess of the approved overdraft level. It also greatly exceeded the level of the only formal security offered by the Trust in the form of the title deeds of some unmortgaged housing properties. The bank manager was frequently telephoning to enquire when payment of the promised Revenue Deficit Grant would be received. For his part, the Trust's case-hardened accountant, Martin Prater, was frequently calling the DoE with a similar question. The only other security that he could offer the bank was a verbal assurance of the authenticity of the verbal messages he was receiving from the DoE that payment would be made shortly.

Martin gives a graphic account of how payment was eventually made:

"The DoE reached the stage of promising to pay the cheque in the week preceding the 1976 August Bank Holiday weekend, but it had not arrived by the Friday. That weekend saw the most 'boisterous' Notting Hill Carnival to date. The windows of the Trust offices in All Saints Road were boarded up as a precaution on

the preceding Friday. Coming to work in the office on the Tuesday meant crunching through broken glass and heaps of litter".

When the post came, the postman brought an insignificant small brown window envelope, containing the note on behalf of the Paymaster General ordering the payment of £1,209,841 to the Trust. Initially the person opening the post did not realise its importance, and when it was opened Martin at first thought it had not been signed, because the signature was such a tiny scrawl in the bottom corner of the note.

When the bank manager was told, rather than let anyone from the Trust come to the bank, he insisted on coming by car for the 500 yard journey from Ladbroke Grove. Given the state of the post-Carnival roads, for added precaution he brought his assistant manager with him. Having taken the cheque he disappeared quickly back to the bank, and put the cheque in to express clearing. Much to everyone's relief, it did not bounce.

The payment to the Trust was the largest payment of Revenue Deficit Grant that had been given. It was very important in putting the Trust's finances on a sound footing.

Frost damage

In 1978 and again in 1981, when fully stretched administratively and financially by a programme completing an average 14 individual property conversions weekly, the Trust was hit by an unprecedented problem requiring urgent action: bad weather.

Its scale may be judged from the fact that ultimately over £2 million had to be found to cope with it. During the winter of 1978-79, later dubbed the "winter of discontent" for the number of strikes during bleak weather, there was one, never-to-be-forgotten, three day period when a number of chunks of cement-like material detached themselves from the tall stuccoed properties in the Colville/Tavistock area of Notting Hill. The properties had been built in the 1860s, so they were almost 120 years old.

The cause of the damage was a period of exceptionally heavy rain, followed by freezing weather. Water got in behind the stucco at the level of parapets, which then froze, and pushed lumps of masonry into the gardens and the street below.

Immediate action was clearly necessary as large chunks of masonry fell onto the pavements in front of the houses. Several were as large as 2 or 3 feet long and very heavy. It was potentially lethal to both tenants and passers-by. In addition to clearing the fallen masonry, a vehicle with a hydraulic lifting platform was required to check all remaining stucco surfaces and to remove any found to be insecure. The difficult bit, however, was still to come!

An emergency repair programme was undertaken during the summer months in 1979. This was a mammoth task, involving coordination by the maintenance team with some 600 tenants whose homes were being repaired, as well as a small army of contractors. Initial estimates indicated prospective remedial costs of the order of £1 million.

By now there had been a change of government and the new housing minister was John Stanley, a close lieutenant of Margaret Thatcher, anxious to win his spurs as a no-nonsense, new broom. There appeared to be no understanding in the Department of the Environment of how or why this episode had happened, nor of what would be required to put it right in such a way as to prevent re-occurrence; nor - perhaps the stickiest question of all - where the money to pay for the work needed was to come from. All suggestion of public funding received dusty answers: *"It's your problem, you solve it"*.

John Coward recalls that:

"It was immediately assumed in high places that such events had occurred as a result of some technical negligence. The Trust's Chairman, Roger Ormrod and I were summoned to the Marsham Street tower (the head offices of the Department of the Environment) and subjected to a humiliating discourse by the Minister accompanied by his principal civil servants sitting in a row – as if in a tribunal."

To defend itself against criticisms of negligence the Trust engaged the expertise of the Building Research Establishment, the Government's own technical agency. Fortunately, they upheld the view that the Trust could not have anticipated the extensive damage to the properties.

Agreement on the funding of remedial works took over four years to resolve, by which time there had been further extensive frost damage in the winter of 1981/2, bringing the total repairs cost to over £2.1 million.

£1,300,000 was eventually met through the payment of Housing Association Grant, and £275,000 under the insurance policy. The Trust paid £573,000 from its own resources, including £143,000 from the sale of properties owned by the Trust, with the first "forced sale" being at 34 Norland Square after the tenants had been re-housed.

The problem with frost damage highlighted the unforeseen hazards which could be experienced with large, 19th century properties, especially those with features such as stucco, and the financial difficulties faced by housing associations without any sources of money to remedy the damage.

The funding arrangements of the 1974 Housing Act, relic of a bipartisan political moment, were based on subsidy for the renovation of properties acquired by housing associations. There was no provision for unexpected remedial work that might suddenly become necessary in future years. This may explain the belligerent attitudes of Ministers and DoE officials, who usually had very co-operative relations with the Trust, when asked for financial help.

In the years that followed many more associations ran into problems with the need for remedial work and re-improvement, even if not of such a sudden and spectacular kind as the Trust experienced. In response, policies and funding arrangements were devised by the Housing Corporation and DoE to cope with these. The frost damage saga was one more example of the Trust being the first to encounter a problem and then to negotiate a solution.

How it might have been different
By the end of the 1970s housing associations had established themselves as a "third arm" in housing provision, with a distinctive character and strengths. The conference of the National Federation of Housing Associations was seen as the annual "get together" of the housing association "movement", responding with excitement or anger respectively, to new opportunities or threats, and inspired by Richard Best's leadership.

There were disparate strands within the active membership of the NFHA: large and small, general and specialist. The most important distinction until the end of the 1980s, however, was between the inner city associations, focusing primarily on rehabilitation of older property, and the new build associations, mostly developing estates of housing on greenfield land.

The leading members of the NFHA were drawn largely, if not exclusively, from the inner city associations. Many of the key individuals were directors of these associations, especially in London and Merseyside, who had come into housing associations as part of the new generation in the 1960s. They included the associations which had benefited from Shelter support in the difficult years prior to the 1974 Housing. John Coward and the Notting Hill Housing Trust were influential members of this group.

With hindsight, the way in which housing associations grew in the 1970s can appear as inevitable. In fact, events might have led to very different outcomes. What if Bruce Kenrick had not decided there was a need for another housing association in North Kensington? What if the Trust had not recruited John Coward? What if the new wave of associations had not challenged the domination of the fee-earning housing societies? The list of possibilities can go on.

What is likely – if not probable - is that the future for the areas of inner city housing stress would have been very different. Without the renovation work of associations, the most run-down areas would have been designated by local authorities as incapable of saving and the houses demolished. In contrast, streets of 19th century terraces with the most potential for renovation would have been improved by owner-occupiers and developers engaged in gentrification. The losers would have been low income residents, either forced out by eviction or left in unimproved properties.

The new framework for housing associations in the 1974 Housing Act would not have happened as it did. Without the rehabilitation work pioneered by the inner city associations the Government would not have decided to commit huge public spending to their work.

Many supporters of municipal housing would have welcomed that because there would not have been an alternative to direct local authority provision. There was considerable suspicion, and some hostility, from left-wing politicians, local authority professionals and many community organisations to the growing role of the new breed of housing associations.

After the election of the Conservative Government in 1979, however, a more radical policy would almost certainly have been adopted. What is rarely considered is what would have happened to social housing provision when a Conservative Government was elected in 1979 if there had not been an active housing association sector?

Margaret Thatcher distrusted local authorities and was hostile to any expansion of "municipalisation". It is extremely unlikely that the Conservative Government would have continued to support direct provision of new homes by local authorities. In the absence of a strong housing association movement it seems likely that the Government would have turned to the private sector. The alternative to housing associations would not have been council housing, but some form of profit-driven, privately owned housing. The result would have been less affordable accommodation for low income households, fewer socially balanced communities and even greater polarization than actually occurred in the "loadsamoney" Eighties.

"North Kensington did not burn"

This book began with an account by Mike Phillips of the murder of Kelso Cochrane in 1969, an event which shattered the widespread complacency about race relations in Britain's inner cities. The response of the Methodist Church to those racial tensions led indirectly to Bruce Kenrick's arrival in Notting Hill and the setting up of the Trust.

Over the next twenty years the Trust played an important role in providing better housing for low income residents, both black and white. Its work helped to reduce discrimination by landlords, which forced black tenants to pay much higher rents for less secure and worse quality accommodation, as the 1967 Notting Hill Summer Project Housing Survey showed.

The work of the Trust in buying and improving houses not only prevented the wholesale gentrification the Colville/Tavistock and other areas. It also made it possible to sustain mixed income, multi-ethnic and socially balanced neighbourhoods.

The regeneration of All Saints Road provided space for black-led shops and businesses, as well as renovation of the housing in the street. Located in the heart of Notting Hill, close to the Mangrove restaurant, it was a visible example of the area being improved for the local community, rather than for business and wealthy newcomers from outside.

Other agencies have made vital contributions to making North Kensington an area where black people "belong". The Notting Hill Carnival grew from a small local event in 1965 to the largest street festival in Europe.

In a very different way the Law Centre has challenged the actions of landlords who harassed and illegally evicted private tenants, many of them black. It has also challenged the behaviour of the police, including the widespread practices of "stop and search", disproportionately arresting black people where there were no valid grounds, and refusing to allow those arrested to make contact with a solicitor.

When a number of inner city neighbourhoods, including Brixton, Tottenham and Liverpool Toxteth, erupted in racial violence in the hot summer of 1981, North Kensington did not. Lord Scarman's Inquiry made scathing criticisms of the record of the police, the local authority and many other agencies in Lambeth. Whilst statutory and other agencies were not immune from similar criticisms, the Notting Hill Housing Trust was an agency which could credibly claim it had acted to strengthen racial justice in west London.

Celebrating apparent racial harmony can easily be seen as complacency, especially when made by a white author. Yet it is also important to recognize real achievements. If the events of the late 1950s had been allowed to pass unchallenged, North Kensington could have become a racially divided area, or one where racial harassment and violence became an everyday occurrence. It could have developed as an area where black people constantly felt unsafe, and those with any choice moved away.

There is still serious racial discrimination and racial inequality, which demand constant vigilance and action to achieve racial justice. Yet Notting Hill today is a multi-ethnic community, where black and white people enjoy its racial and cultural diversity. It remains a place where most residents want to live, and is an example – even an icon – for many from outside, not just in Britain but in other countries. The Notting Hill Housing Trust has played an important part in achieving that progress over the past forty years. In a deeply divided world, it is a living example of how people from many different backgrounds can, and should, be able to live together.

Little wonder that the makers of the film, Notting Hill, were easily persuaded to acknowledge their own debt when Mary Harvey, by now director of the Trust's eager fundraising team, approached them. As a result a non-West End premiere was staged at the Coronet Cinema at Notting Hill Gate, ringing the tills for the Trust. Mary even persuaded the distributors of the subsequent video to include a plug for the Trust before the opening credits on every copy.

Chapter 10

A HARSHER CLIMATE

From 1979 onwards the Trust moved into a different era, as a result of the changes stemming from the General Election that led to the defeat of the Labour Government,

The housing priority for the new Conservative Government was expanding home ownership, especially through its flagship "right to buy" policy. More money was allocated to shared ownership schemes, funding for rented homes suffered successive cuts. It became increasingly difficult for housing associations to sustain the inner city rehabilitation programmes which were so successful in the 1970s.

The 1980s saw an increase in poverty and social polarisation. Unemployment grew, especially amongst young people. As more people bought their homes, it was increasingly poorer people who lived in socially rented housing.

The average incomes of households living in social housing fell over ten years from three quarters of the national average in 1980 to less than half (below the European Union poverty threshold) by 1990.

The proportion of social housing tenants at the bottom end of the income scale rose, from half in the lowest 40% of incomes in 1979 to over three quarters by 1994.

In 1975 a quarter of households with the highest 40% of incomes lived in social housing. By 1994 this had dropped to less than 5%.

The biggest legislative change for housing associations came with the 1988 Housing Act. This ushered in the new era of "private finance", with associations borrowing money from private lenders to fund new developments. The Act also ended the role of the Rent Officer in setting rents, so that housing associations themselves fixed the rents for the new tenancies.

Associations could no longer depend on public funds to underpin development and housing management costs. They had to learn new skills in assessing financial risk, to develop robust business plans and to cope in a more competitive environment.

The Notting Hill Housing Trust responded in a range of ways during the 1980s and 1990s. The Addison Housing Association was formed in 1980, to develop an expanding programme of low cost home ownership. A Temporary Housing Unit was set up to provide an alternative to the escalating number of homeless families in bed and breakfast.

The Trust built more new housing estates, which led to some problems which had not been experienced in renovating older properties. It also took on a wider role in regeneration, both with its own properties and in partnership with local authorities.

As a result of the community development approach, which became a key feature in these regeneration projects, the Trust evolved a "vision for neighbourhoods", which underpins how it seeks to work with residents in the range of different communities where it owns and manages homes.

Facing housing cuts

Since the 1974 Housing Act the Trust had enjoyed large annual allocations of funding, especially from the Housing Corporation, to buy and renovate older houses. In 1980 this changed dramatically.

At the September conference of the National Federation of Housing Associations the Housing Minister, John Stanley, announced plans to reduce the funding available in future for rented homes. An immediate six month moratorium was announced on letting any new building contracts funded by the Housing Corporation.

In his introduction to the annual report in March 1981, the Trust's Chairman, Sir Roger Ormrod, spoke out strongly about the consequences of the changed climate:

"My introduction this year must be of a somewhat pessimistic nature in contrast to the more optimistic message of recent annual reports. In the period covered by this report the Trust has experienced change equal, but unfortunately in the opposite direction, to the dramatic change that took place in the second half of the seventies after the passing of the 1974 Act. That Act, more than anything else, heralded a major shift of resources into housing and promoted the expansion of the housing association movement. Government pronouncement and action in the last 18 months have confirmed that that optimistic period is now all but at an end.

The co-operative enterprise through partnership between the Trust and local and national government agencies has achieved the virtual transformation of an area like Notting Hill from a place of decay and deprivation into a reasonable place to live and removed many of the tensions. The Trust would hope this could be maintained and repeated in the future but it is doubtful that government wishes this to be so. The Trust is suffering considerably as a result of the Government's ambivalence".

Similar concerns were expressed in the lead letter in the Times published on September 11 1981. It was written by John Coward shortly after violent racial disturbances in Brixton, Bristol and Liverpool which created public alarm about the serious problems in inner city areas. The annual Notting Hill Carnival had also taken place a few days earlier.

"Sir, The contrast between the recent riots in inner city areas and the success of the Notting Hill Carnival is very relevant to the review of the situation in the inner cities being undertaken by ministers, especially by Mr. Heseltine. Since the early seventies housing associations in this area have been working vigorously buying and rehabilitating the mass of old decaying houses and handling the human problems involved, thus countering the general deterioration and demoralisation which is otherwise inevitable.

In this work they have hitherto received the practical support of both political parties... Housing associations, in cooperation with local authorities, have been able to make a significant impact on this problem. In areas like Notting Hill the work has been concentrated and effective.

It is sad that over the last two years there has been a substantial reduction in the programmes of housing associations engaged in this vital work. Whilst government support for housing association activity has been maintained this year at the 1980/1 level resources, there has been a significant shift of resources away from work in stress areas to other aspects of housing provision. Associations working with the poorer sections of the community feel more and more that their work no longer attracts the support of government and is no longer seen as a priority."

What is striking about Roger Ormrod's statement and John Coward's letter are their confident claims about the impact made by the association's work over the past few years, and the strength of their belief that this work was suffering seriously because of the reduction in government support.

The NFHA organised a very high profile campaign to publicise the impact of the cuts in the Housing Corporation's budget, especially the moratorium on letting any rehabilitation contracts. The highlight of the campaign was the participation of 29 Anglican bishops in an impressively orchestrated publicity event, with each bishop being photographed outside a house that could not be improved because of the moratorium.

Almost certainly as a result of this intensive lobbying, the subsequent cuts to the Housing Corporation's programme were lower than had been expected. However, the different priorities of the Conservative Government meant that there was less money for work in areas with the worst housing problems.

In the period from the early 1970s until 1979 inner city housing associations like Notting Hill had benefited from Government policies that were favourable to their work. From 1980 onwards this changed, and the Trust found itself working against the grain of the Thatcher Government's policies and the dominant political attitudes.

By the end of the 1980s Housing Corporation funding for rehabilitation had virtually ended. Although there were still serious problems of disrepair and multi-occupation, many of the worst properties in the Trust's area of operation had been improved, either by the Trust or private owners. Rising house prices were making it impossible to buy and renovate properties within the Housing Corporation's budgetary constraints.

In addition, funding priorities were changing. More local authority funding was being used for work on their own housing stock. More of the Housing Corporation's budget was being allocated to shared ownership.

When the bipartisan 1974 Housing Act had come into force new developments by housing associations were funded by a form of deficit financing. They received a loan from the Housing Corporation, repayable from rental income, and a payment of Housing Association Grant to meet all the capital costs which could not be funded from the rental income. As associations could only charge the "fair rents" set by the Rent Officer, the Housing Association Grant was needed to cover most of the costs. The average grant was between 70% and 80%, and still higher in many inner city areas.

This arrangement was very attractive. The particular form of the Housing Association Grant (HAG) subsidy gave an extra – and probably unintended – benefit to housing associations. HAG was given in a lump sum at the point when the development work was completed, with the calculation that rent income would be sufficient to meet all outstanding costs. However the new arrangements came in at a time of uniquely high inflation, peaking at 25%. It meant that rents tended to rise in line with prices, while loan repayments which were on a fixed interest rate, stayed the same. The result was that surpluses started to accrue to housing associations.

The HAG system was devised at the time when government policy was to boost housing association activity and when there were far fewer constraints on government spending. After public spending constraints became much tighter after the 1976 financial crisis, HAG was increasingly seen as extravagant.

In retrospect, it may seem surprising that the Government introduced such a generous scheme. It had not been expected that housing association activity would expand so much or so fast. The unpredicted result, was that, at a time when support for tax cuts and the pressure to cut public spending was growing, the cost of housing association subsidy was seen by government ministers as unsustainably high.

Another disadvantage of the funding system was that associations had no incentive to contain costs. The Housing Corporation and local authority funders exercised detailed controls on what building work was eligible for subsidy, but for associations lower costs simply meant less grant. The funding system was also expensive in its public spending implications as not only the subsidy, but also the mortgage, counted against the Public Spending Borrowing Requirement, the critical measure of public spending.

The 1988 Housing Act

By the mid-1980s the Government was preparing legislation that would radically change the financial framework within which housing associations would provide new homes. The 1988 Housing Act was a major watershed for housing associations. The Government's aim was to fund more of the cost of housing association development through private finance, and to reduce the dependence on public funding. To maintain their development programmes in future, housing associations would need to borrow from private lenders.

The only exceptions were black and ethnic minority associations, locally based community associations and special needs schemes which continued to receive loans from the Housing Corporation because it was felt that they were unable to borrow money at competitive terms on the private market.

The 1988 Housing Act also removed the requirement on housing associations to charge "fair rents", which were fixed externally by the Rent Officer. The old system had meant that the level of grant required for a new scheme was determined by the rent set by the Rent Officer. Under the new scheme the Housing Corporation decided on the level of grant. As they chose to set these at a level lower than previously this had the effect that rent levels were higher.

New tenancies were let on "assured tenancies" on which associations decided the rents themselves, rather than them being decided independently by the Rent Officer. This left associations able to raise rents to compensate for the reduced rate of grant.

The benefit to the public purse from the new arrangements was that where loans came from private lenders, rather than the Housing Corporation, this did not count as public spending. That was a plus for the Treasury as it struggled to contain such expenditure, a central priority for Mrs Thatcher. The attraction for associations was that if the Government maintained the level of Housing Corporation funding at the same level as before this would enable more new homes to be developed for the same amount of public money.

The problem for housing associations was that the new arrangements gave a clear way of reducing the level of public subsidy needed for an individual scheme. Associations were asked to limit the requirement for grant on new schemes, both by charging higher rents and by reducing costs. It became the practice to force associations to compete for development opportunities, with the winner being the association applying for the lowest level of grant.

Funding for development activity increasingly went to larger associations, especially those with reserves, which could subsidise new housing schemes. Those who benefited most were the stock transfer associations with reserves derived from capital receipts from right to buy sales to tenants.

While the stricter financial framework has led to tighter cost control and efficiency savings, it has also led to examples of associations reducing costs by cutting standards and only developing on cheaper sites. This enabled more schemes to be built from the total budget available, but it has also meant that more new homes have been built in less attractive neighbourhoods, and with the elimination of features considered inessential, even where they would have enhanced the quality of the new homes and their environment.

Following the 1988 Act total capital expenditure by housing associations rose sharply, from £1,009 million in 1988/9 to a peak of £3,608 million in 1992/3. However it then fell progressively each year to £1,849 million in 1997/8.

The increase in the earlier years was the result of both the injection of private finance and also an increase in public spending, as the Government responded to the rising levels of homelessness and the collapse of the housing market.

What the supporters of the use of private finance can justifiably claim is that from the early 1990s the new arrangements have resulted in spending on housing association investment consistently being at least £1,000 million a year higher than it would otherwise have been. In practice, private borrowing has complemented public subsidy, and not reduced it.

Rising rents

However, the new financial arrangements did lead to sharp increases in the rents for newly built accommodation, as the Housing Corporation reduced grant rates. The Trust publicly expressed their concerns at this prospect in their annual report for 1990/1:

"Our central objective is to provide good quality homes for those on low incomes at rents they can afford. There is now the risk that grant rates will be reduced to a level at which we cannot achieve this objective. Over the last five years there has already been a substantial reduction in average grant rates.

We have been able to accommodate these reductions partly by raising rents by 56% (a real increase of 22%) and partly by the unprecedented fall in land prices and construction costs. We do not think that substantial further rent increases can be justified. Such increases virtually force those tenants to give up work. The reduction in grant rates also threatens our ability to raise funds in the private market. If grant rates fall further both capital cover for our borrowings and security of rental income will be placed in jeopardy. We have joined with associations across the country in campaigning vigorously against further reductions in grant rates".

Higher rents led to considerable concern amongst associations. However, the Government seemed unconcerned. When asked to justify the policy the Housing Minister, Sir George Young, replied *"We'll let housing benefit take the strain".* He meant that where tenants could not afford the higher rents, they could get financial help from claiming housing benefit. This reply ignored the risk that tenants would be caught in a trap where they were no better off if they got a job than when they were unemployed.

Ironically, the Tory determination to shift housing subsidy away from "bricks and mortar" to the direct subsidy of needy individuals during this phase of policy had a less welcome consequence for cost-cutting ministers. As poverty and low wages, relative and absolute, expanded in many market-sensitive sectors so did legitimate claims for housing benefit. By the end of the 18 years of Conservative rule it was costing upwards of a £1 billion a year.

Another challenge the Trust faced was a growing difficulty in providing new homes in its traditional core areas, especially Kensington and Chelsea and Hammersmith and Fulham. There was ever greater pressure to increase volume by moving to more peripheral and, consequently, cheaper areas on the fringes of London. The Annual Report commented:

"Too often this pressure seems to place numbers before the needs of the people and communities we have traditionally served. Rehabilitation work in the inner city has virtually ceased."

Election of a Labour Government

When the Labour Government was elected in May 1997 funding for housing association investment was about to fall to the lowest level for twenty years, as a result of the outgoing Tory Chancellor, Kenneth Clarke's, budget cuts the previous November. The policy of the Labour Government was to support more investment in social housing, but the new Chancellor, Gordon Brown's, pre-election commitment to stay within the Conservative spending limits meant there was no extra money for housing associations.

On entering office the new Government's housing priorities focused on tackling issues of low demand. But a belated awareness of the acute housing shortage in southern England, the escalating numbers of homeless families in bed and breakfast accommodation, and the difficulties key workers faced in finding affordable homes led to a review of priorities.

New thinking was reflected in the Housing Policy Green Paper published in April 2000. It was followed by the Spending Review three months later, and the announcement of the Communities Plan in February 2002. Key proposals in the Plan were in the Thames Gateway, and three major "growth areas" in the southeast around Milton Keynes, Stansted in Essex and Ashford in Kent.

The following summer Chancellor Brown commissioned one of his economic advisers from the Bank of England, Kate Barker, to carry out a review of housing supply and the economic effects of problems in the housing market. Her two reports provided powerful evidence that too few new homes had been built in southern England for more than twenty years, and that under-supply was the major cause of high house prices and worsening problems of affordability.

The cumulative result of these events was that housing started to become a higher political priority. The Housing Corporation budget rose from £541 million in 1997/8 to over £2,000 million by 2004/5, with further increases projected in the 2004 Spending Review for future years.

London's elected Mayor, Ken Livingstone, published the statutory Plan for London which set an ambitious target of 30,000 new homes a year, with the proviso that 35% of all new homes should be for social renting, and 15% for people on middle incomes who could not afford market prices, especially "key workers" in public services.

Major changes for the Trust
Within the Trust there were major changes. In 1986 John Coward retired. Two years later Sir Roger Ormrod stood down after almost twenty years as Chair. Together they had guided the Trust through an extraordinary time of innovation and growth, complementing each other by their different roles and personalities. They had constituted the rock on which the Trust had stood, firm against threats and true to the vision which had inspired the Trust's founders.

Donald Hoodless was appointed as the new Chief Executive. He had been the Director of Circle 33 Housing Trust since 1974, as well as having been a councillor in Islington for many years and served as Labour Leader of the Council. He was well placed to lead the Trust into a new era.

Anthony Taussig succeeded Roger Ormrod as the Chair in 1988. He had been a member of the Board for twenty years, and had also been a member of the North Kensington Area Committee since it was set up, as well as Chair of Notting Hill Commercial Properties and Addison Housing Association.

The Trust had started to borrow from private lenders even before the new Housing Act came into force, and had raised £80 million between 1985 and 1988. The largest single loan was £27 million for a leaseback arrangement at

Drayton Bridge in Ealing, to buy an estate of 252 newly built homes from Barratts. It had to be negotiated under a very tight timetable to allow the purchase to be completed before new Government regulations came into force which ended the subsidy benefits hitherto available for this kind of leaseback. This deal was controversial within the Trust, but Donald Hoodless saw it as evidence that the Trust could be successful in negotiating a large and complex agreement for new development.

A Tenants Survey carried out in 1993 showed encouraging levels of satisfaction with services being provided by the Trust. No less than 86% of tenants described the Trust as a good landlord, and 78% said they were satisfied with their home. An overwhelming majority (91%) said that they would choose the Trust as their landlord.

However, after seven years at Notting Hill, Donald Hoodless resigned as Chief Executive in late 1993 to return to his old post at Circle 33. During his time with the Trust, 3,500 homes had been completed, in addition to the properties leased from private owners for homeless households. He had steered the organisation through huge changes, including new legislation, different funding arrangements, and the development of large, new build housing estates. Sue Black believes *"Donald was a very good manager. He was incredibly supportive and trusted you to get on with it"*.

In 1994 Anthony Taussig was succeeded as Chair by Lionel Morrison, who had been a member of the Committee of Management since 1979, and also a member of the North Kensington Area Committee.

Chapter 11

BUILDING NEW ESTATES

Over its first twenty years almost all the Trust's development activity had been in rehabilitating street properties. In a few areas there was a concentration of properties in the same neighbourhood, such as the Colville/Powis area in North Kensington, but the Trust did not own what would be called an "estate" of the kind which local authorities commonly had built. In the late 1980s this started to change.

The Trust's first large, new build housing estate was the Drayton Bridge project in Ealing, a development of 252 rented homes bought by the Trust from the builders Barratt's and leased back to the local authority. This was one of the first such schemes, set up in this way to avoid the capital restrictions placed by the Government on local authorities. As the money to build the homes was borrowed by the housing association there was no capital cost to the Council. Instead it paid revenue payments to the housing association to meet the repayment costs on the loan they had taken out.

Ealing Council had devised the project in response to the growing number of homeless families in costly and unsatisfactory bed and breakfast (B & B) accommodation. Its value was in providing long-term settled homes, at a cheaper cost. In recognition of the funding arrangements, the Trust agreed to grant 100% nominations to the local authority. It was the first time that such a high level of nominations had been agreed.

Unfortunately there were serious difficulties with the management of the estate, resulting from the high proportion of children and a heavy concentration of vulnerable residents. In effect it had been "bought off the shelf", with no prior input from the association into its design and specification. The management agreement with the Council left the Trust with no control over lettings.

In the early 1990's the Trust built five estates with more than 100 homes each. These were:

Windmill Park, LB Ealing	500 homes
Rootes, RB Kensington and Chelsea	281 "
Lithos Road, LB Camden	158 "
Perivale, LB Ealing	153 "
West Middlesex Hospital, LB Hounslow	140 "

The second large estate development was at Lithos Road in Camden, where the Trust built 158 homes in a consortium with three other associations. These were Circle 33, West Hampstead Housing Association and Odu-Dua, a small, black African-led association based in Camden.

This was the Trust's first experience of managing an estate in a consortium. The new practice reflected the policy of the Housing Corporation during that period, which was to encourage active competition between associations for new development opportunities, but also frequently to offer funding for a new scheme to several associations provided they bid together. Its positive benefit was that it provided opportunities for small associations to share in development opportunities on larger sites, which would not have possible for them on their own. Its drawbacks were that little thought seems to have been given to the complexities of providing good and cost-effective management services post construction.

Like many housing associations the Trust was unhappy with this policy, as the need to liaise with other partners, and the inevitable duplication of some activities, increased costs. Housing management costs were higher if separate associations were separately managing only a small number of units. There was also a risk of tension, leading to outright disagreement, where associations had different policies or differed on how to deal with a particular problem.

The largest such estate developed by the Trust was at Windmill Park, on land previously used by St Bernard's Hospital. In line with the Housing Corporation policy the homes were developed by eleven different social landlords, of which the Notting Hill Housing Trust and Ealing Family Housing Association were the two largest.

Rod Cahill, now Chief Executive of Ealing Family Housing Association, believes that the fragmentation of ownership has been the cause of many of the management difficulties on the estate, and resolved not to enter into any similar arrangements in the future.

Building new communities
In 1993 the Joseph Rowntree Foundation published a seminal report "Building Communities"[1] based on a study of new housing association

estates carried out by David Page. The stimulus to the project had come from a growing concern about the management problems being experienced on some of the newly built estates completed by housing associations. One of the case studies for the research was the Trust's Drayton Bridge estate, although it was described under the pseudonym of "St Anthony's" (the use of the first name of the Trust's Chair may have been a mischievous pun or simply coincidence!).

The Rowntree report described the major changes in the development programmes of housing associations which had taken place in recent years, especially the shift from the rehabilitation of inner city street houses to building purpose built, new housing estates.

It also highlighted the dramatic social changes which had taken place during the 1980s. At the beginning of the decade the average income of council tenants was 73% of the national average. By 1990 this had fallen to 48%, whilst for housing association tenants it was only 45% of average national income.

The publication of David Page's report was a significant landmark for housing associations. Until the end of the 1980s housing associations owned relatively few large estates. They had avoided building high rise or deck access flats. They had not experienced the dramatic decline of estates, which was seen as a problem peculiar to local authorities. To their dismay they found that they were experiencing similar difficulties.

A key finding of the research was the significance of the high child densities, especially where there was a high proportion of two bedroom or larger flats. On the Drayton Bridge estate the local authority had 100% nomination rights and these were used almost wholly to re-house homeless families from temporary accommodation. It was estimated that 55% of all residents were children.

Research had also shown that there was a strong correlation between the extent of vandalism and the numbers of young children, which had led to recommendations that not more than 25% of all residents should be children.

The study of new estates also showed that their design and layout did not prevent vandalism and crime. In her famous book, the "Life and Death of Great American Cities", Jane Jacobs argues that what makes neighbourhoods safe are "eyes on the street", from people looking out of their windows or walking up or down.

The research found that whilst some of the estates designed by architects showed a considerable awareness of safety in their design, the "off the shelf" schemes bought from house builders showed many of the failings of poor layout. Criticisms of the Drayton Bridge estate included isolated car parking space, unlit footpaths and other vulnerable areas.

Finally, some associations had failed to recognise the importance of having a local housing management presence. On an estate the landlord has more responsibilities than for an individual street property. These may include the cleaning and removal of rubbish from common areas, cutting the grass, and ensuring controlled entry systems, lifts and lighting are working well.

If an estate is well looked after, tenants are more likely to support the efforts of the landlord and want to share responsibility for keeping up standards. If it is not looked after well, tenants rapidly become dissatisfied and pride in the estate falls. The Drayton Bridge estate had acquired a bad reputation within two years of the first lettings.

The Rowntree report received widespread publicity. In the sometimes frenetic debate which followed its publication some associations jumped to over-simplistic conclusions. They saw the cause of the problem as too many homeless families, and blamed local authorities for nominating too high a proportion of lettings to new estates. Some commentators went still further. That housing associations were facing the same problems as local authorities was seen as evidence of *"the stigma of social housing"*. Their conclusion was that social housing had failed.

Fortunately, the Trust and most other associations adopted a different response, helped by the recommendations in David Page's report drawn from successful policies already being followed by some local authorities and housing associations. It was recognised that housing estates are fundamentally different from street properties, and that this had important implications for how they should be managed. It also led to a design philosophy whereby more effort was made to reduce the "estateness" feel of estates, for example by creating traditional street patterns.

For its next major development the Trust resolved to apply the lessons learnt. A site previously occupied by the Rootes Car factory was bought to build 223 homes for rent and 73 for shared ownership. It was the largest development of new social housing in Kensington for over thirty years.

The Trust was the lead housing association in a consortium with three other associations. Jointly they set out their vision for the estate, moving away from traditional approaches to design and promoting a socially balanced community. An Estate Agreement was signed by the associations, setting out how they would work together. This was a unique arrangement between housing associations sharing responsibility for the management of the estate.

The design of the estate reflected the belief *"that a new estate should fit in with the surrounding neighbourhood looking out, not turning its back on the community"*. A mix of dwellings was provided to bring together a variety of household types. Twenty one flats had wheelchair access. To provide opportunities for employment 20,000 square feet of commercial space were turned into 50 light industrial workshops and made available for rent to local start-up businesses.

The mix of residents contained a spread of households of different sizes, and with a range of income levels. Lettings were carefully managed to prevent too large a future population of children of the same age. A resettlement worker helped those who needed assistance move into their new homes, and also identified tenants requiring long term support.

Addison Housing Association, now known as Notting Hill Home Ownership, worked very closely with the Borough to meet housing need. Where previously most shared owners had applied directly to the association, in this case over 50 per cent were Borough nominations.

Suggestions from local residents, tenants living on nearby estates and neighbourhood groups led to the creation of the new community facilities. These included a residents' association office and meeting facilities, a doctor's practice, two youth projects, the Youth Cable TV Workshop to train young people in television production and Sound Arts to teach children to play, sing and listen to music.

An artist ran a community project with the aim of adding visual interest. Groups of former Rootes employees, local sheltered housing residents, school children and Mencap members, each designed a mosaic relevant to the history of the site. These were mounted on the external gables and walls for residents and visitors to see. A community development manager was employed to co-ordinate all these projects.

In developing these proposals for the Rootes estate, however, the Trust had not initially foreseen the wider needs of the community, in what was an isolated area in the far north-west of the Borough. In total there were 1,800 flats on estates owned by eight housing associations. These included the Peabody and William Sutton Trusts, which owned two large estates of walk-up flats.

A review of the community needs showed a serious lack of community facilities, little provision for young people, and high levels of youth unemployment, especially amongst young people. A successful bid was made for a six year programme of funding from the Single Regeneration Budget (SRB) for the "Dalgarno Wedge", which was the name chosen for the group of estates, after one of the roads and estates in the centre of the area. A review carried out after the first two years found that the project had achieved *"substantial successes"* and *"put Dalgarno on the map"*.

One issue identified by residents was the need for greater co-ordination between the different landlords managing the Dalgarno neighbourhood.

Consultation with residents identified all-too-familiar urban problems such as poor street sweeping, bulky refuse collection and grounds maintenance. A Neighbourhood Management Action Plan was drawn up, but there were persistent problems in securing firm commitment to it from all the housing associations, despite the allocation of £100,000 funding to employ a Neighbourhood Manager for two years.

Steve Hilditch was appointed the Chair of the Dalgarno Project. He had become a member of the Kensington Area Committee of the Trust in 1988, and four years later became a member of the Board. He has many years experience as a senior housing professional and is a seasoned community campaigner.

His CV includes being Shelter's Head of Policy and Secretary of the Westminster Objectors Trust. As such he helped bring about the investigations which led to Lady Shirley Porter, the former Leader of Westminster City Council, being surcharged for "gerrymandering" the Council's housing policy for party political gain, at the expense of homeless families.

He sees the Dalgarno project as an important way in which the Trust can work with residents of different housing associations to improve the quality of life in the area. However, he has been disappointed at the way in which all the housing associations, including the Trust's own housing services division, have *"dragged their feet"* in providing integrated neighbourhood management covering all the estates.

In response to the frustration of the tenants, the local Labour MP for Regents Park and Kensington North, Karen Buck, convened a meeting at the House of Commons to which she asked the chief executives from all the housing associations. As a result agreement was reached at last, which led to the recruitment of the Neighbourhood Manager.

Grahame Park

The most ambitious project currently being planned by the Group is at Grahame Park in Barnet. This contains a number of elements which are likely to characterise other developments in the future: working in a neighbourhood with high levels of deprivation, improving the quality of housing, developing a socially mixed community, using the proceeds from market sales to subsidize socially rented housing and seeking alternatives to Social Housing Grant.

Grahame Park is a 1777 dwelling council estate in Colindale, northwest London. It was built on the now discredited Radburn design system, the separation of cars and pedestrians, with roads and car parks fringing the estate and a maze of pedestrian pathways.

The housing is a mixture of small terraces of houses and long blocks of flats divided by walkways and common stairwells. The estate has been unpopular since first letting. High tenancy turnover and lettings difficulties have meant that applicants with the least choice are given housing on Grahame Park and this has led over the years to an excessive concentration of poverty and disadvantage.

As a result of the Council's allocations policy, the estate has a very young population, with nearly half of all residents under 25 years old. Anti-social behaviour, drug and alcohol abuse and fear of crime are prevalent. The quality of the housing is poor with obsolete facilities and ageing fabric, and there is a high level of overcrowding. Outbreaks of multiple infestation are common. The flats suffer from poor acoustic and thermal performance, which further damage the quality of life for residents.

The Group bid for the project in partnership with the Genesis Group. A key reason for this was the shared history of Notting Hill and Paddington Churches Housing Association, and their belief this would help in developing an agreed way of working.

A Master Plan has been drawn up, with proposals to:

- Demolish three-quarters of the estate – 1,317 homes – in phases over a twelve year period.
- Remodel the estate with traditional streets, a new centre and enhanced open spaces.
- Build 2,977 homes, including 1,977 for sale and 1,000 for rent or shared ownership, as well as the public buildings and shops.
- Support the establishment of a community development trust to promote socio-economic programmes by, and for the benefit of, the community.

As the development will replace existing local authority housing, it is not eligible for social housing grant, and will not receive any public subsidy except the transfer of the land to the housing association partnership without payment. To be financially viable, the sales of the owner-occupied properties will need to cover the total cost of the redevelopment of the existing council estate and building of the affordable homes.

Existing residents of Grahame Park are seen as key stakeholders in the regeneration. Residents are intensively involved in the regeneration programme, and were involved in the selection of Choices for Grahame Park (CfGP) by the Council. Residents:

- Joined with CfGP in the selection of Countryside Properties as the housebuilder partner.

- Set up the Grahame Park Neighbourhood Panel to work with CfGP on the regeneration project.
- Negotiated with them on key elements – examples were discussions on the tenancy agreement and lettings policy.
- Participated in design groups, exhibitions, fun-days and area meetings.
- Hold four places on the Interim Partnership Board, where residents' reports are regularly presented for discussion.

In June 2003, 68 per cent of residents voted on the proposals, and 79 per cent of those voted "yes". Both the level of turnout and approval compare favourably with the votes on stock transfer proposals in other areas.

1. *Building Communities, David Page, Joseph Rowntree Foundation, 1993.*

Chapter 12

MOVING INTO A NEW ERA

Low cost home ownership

Extending home ownership was a top priority for Margaret Thatcher and her Government on their election in 1979. Giving council tenants the "right to buy" became one of Thatcherism's flagship policies, although when it was first introduced by her Environment Secretary, Michael Heseltine, it did not have the symbolic importance it later acquired.

The generous discounts made buying their home very popular with tenants, and over one and a half million tenants bought them in the subsequent twenty years. Shared ownership was seen as another means of extending access to home ownership for people who were not council tenants eligible for the right to buy and who could not afford to buy a property outright.

John Stanley, the new Housing Minister, who had been Mrs Thatcher's parliamentary private secretary in Opposition, was already a keen advocate of shared ownership. He had written a pamphlet published by the Conservative Political Centre as early as in 1974, with an introduction by Mrs Thatcher who was then Shadow Secretary of State for the Environment. This put the case for promoting shared ownership so as to enable people who could not afford to buy outright to gain access to a first rung of home ownership.

The attitude of the Conservative Party to housing associations was varied. Some members were active and enthusiastic supporters of housing associations. These included those who had played a long-standing role as committee members of associations, such as Lord Burleigh and Councillor Diana Paul in the Kensington Housing Trust, as well as those who had become active in the newer generation of associations. Another strong supporter was Sir George Young, Conservative MP for Ealing Acton in west London, one of the boroughs where the Trust was actively working.

There were other Tory MPs whose support for housing associations was more guarded. They were strongly critical of council housing, which was seen as inefficient, wasteful and paternalistic. As a sensitive teenager living in a multi-occupied rented house in Brixton, John Major, the next Conservative Prime Minister, was one of them. Housing associations were seen as voluntary organisations, which offered a much preferable alternative to direct provision by local authorities. However, some of those who were aware of associations' heavy reliance on public subsidy were critical. They had fears that this could be municipal housing "through the back door".

But just as the Trust had been obliged to fight barely-veiled hostility from Conservative traditionalists in Kensington and Chelsea in the early days, so housing associations faced significant opposition within the Labour Party, especially at the local level. Many Labour Party members believed that local councils should be the sole providers of rented housing and only supported housing associations where they were providing an extra source of affordable homes. They tended to be very sceptical, if not outright hostile, to housing associations providing anything except rented accommodation.

Trying to contain rising levels of public spending was a major priority for the Thatcher Government, and cuts were made in the Housing Corporation budget from 1980/81 onwards. However, the home ownership programme was protected from these cuts and funding steadily grew, albeit from a very small base.

In 1981 the Trust became one of the first associations to create a separate subsidiary for this type of work. It named it the Addison Housing Association, after a street in Kensington, which was thought to be an appropriate alternative to Notting Hill in the north of the borough. However, Andrew Williamson insists the name was chosen because Addison begins with an "a", so that when its staff went to conferences or other events, their name would come first in any list of attendees! It was a simple idea, but one that works.

Over the next few years Addison developed a range of low cost home ownership programmes. As well as shared ownership, these included leasehold schemes for the elderly, improvement for sale schemes and Do It Yourself Shared Ownership (DIYSO). This was a scheme which enabled applicants to identify the property in which they wanted to live and the association would seek it to purchase it, provided a shared ownership scheme could be developed within the agreed cost limits.

Initially, the Trust had developed shared ownership on a 50:50 basis, with no option to increase the privately owned share. The Conservative Government wanted all leaseholders to be able to increase their equity share, and as a result "staircasing" was incorporated in all new schemes.

This meant properties could be taken out of shared ownership and become part of the normal housing market. However, the association benefited financially from selling the equity share, especially as property prices were rising.

When interest rates soared following the 1988 Budget, as Nigel Lawson's election-winning boom spiralled out of control, there was an alarming growth in mortgage arrears. In response to this, Addison Housing Association was one of the first to introduce an option for leaseholders to "staircase" downwards, by reducing the share they owned in order to make mortgage repayments more affordable. The advantage was that although the rent element increased, this payment was eligible for housing benefit, so that the overall cost payable by the leaseholder was reduced. As a result, for some people, this was successful in reducing the growth of arrears, and the potential risk of repossession.

Nationally, however, repossessions by lenders grew to unprecedented levels, and reached a peak of over 70,000 repossessions in 1992. The Trust found itself being asked to respond to a new form of housing need, re-housing former owner-occupiers whose homes had been repossessed.

Geeta Ahluwalia was one home owner who lost everything when her husband's business went bankrupt and their marriage collapsed. Their house was repossessed, and Geeta went to stay with relatives in the United States. However, she was unhappy there and came back to England. At first she stayed with friends, and then went to the Council to apply for housing as a homeless person. Geeta was shocked by the attitudes she encountered, including being accused of hiding money.

Geeta was placed in a bed and breakfast hotel in Hanwell, and then moved to another hotel, before eventually being nominated for re-housing to the Trust. Now she lives in Sidney Miller house, a sheltered housing scheme in Acton, named after the Trust's long-serving committee member.

Like many people who lost their home through mortgage repossession Geeta *"couldn't believe that I could become homeless"*. Although she is now happy in her new home, she found the experience traumatic and humiliating.

Housing stock investment and regeneration

By the early 1990s the Trust faced another large and growing problem - that of serious dilapidation and obsolescence in many of the properties it had acquired in the heroic pioneer days of hand-to-mouth existence.

Recognition of the seriousness of the problem came as a result of pressure exerted by the Area Committees, especially by tenant representatives. They had been raising the issue for some time, but initially little action had been taken.

By the early 1990s, however, conditions, in approximately 700 flats were unacceptable. This was partly the result of the lower standards of conversion work on properties which had been rehabilitated up to 25 years earlier. In more recent years the problem had been allowed to develop because priority had been given to investing in new housing projects, not to work on the Trust's existing homes. There had not been a separate budget for major repairs and reimprovement, yet despite this, maintenance costs were rising steeply.

Some renewal work was being carried out, but on an ad hoc basis. Yet the amount spent was limited by the extent of any surplus in the Trust's annual revenue account. This approach was palpably failing to respond to an increasingly acute problem. The Trust's prized and hard-won reputation was being damaged in the eyes of its tenants and among the local authorities.

To assist in tackling this problem John Coward was invited to join the Board in 1993 and asked to lead a working party, which included tenant and other members of the Committee, together with staff members. After commissioning external consultants to carry out surveys to establish the number and the condition of houses requiring major work, and estimate the cost, the working party recommended:

a) In view of the very large backlog, re-improvement work should be carried out in a 10 year programme. The costs over the 10 years were estimated at £110 million, or £11 million of expenditure each year.

b) The previous practice of limiting essential works to the anticipated revenue surpluses in any one year should be replaced with an annual budget to meet the costs of fully implementing the re-investment programme.

c) If necessary, property should be sold year by year to provide sufficient funds for the programme. This was felt to be a powerful stimulus to efficiency!

These recommendations were approved by the Committee. They resulted, not only in major stock improvement, but also in changes in the culture and processes of the organisation to ensure continuous future updating of housing stock on a programmed basis. It was a significant acknowledgment of the recurring need to re-evaluate the Trust's shifting priorities.

Progress on the programme was reviewed by the Board in 2002. In 1995 it was anticipated that some 4700 homes out of a total of 8500 in management at that time, would require significant funds to be spent on major repairs, the provision of modern amenities and energy efficiency measures. By 2002 £73 million had been spent and 3250 homes had been improved. 131 housing units had been sold, a significant number, but representing less than 1% of the vacant possession value of the Trust's holdings.

The Colville Project

One area where the Trust embarked on the improvement of older street properties was the Colville area in North Kensington. This project came to play a key role in its the wider approach to regeneration. The area was one where the Trust had bought and renovated properties from its earliest days, and owned a total of 550 properties. More than half of these had been renovated before the more generous capital funding system brought in by the 1974 Housing Act. Never having been converted to high standards in the first place, hundreds had unsurprisingly fallen into considerable disrepair.

By the early 1990s, the area was suffering from a number of serious problems. Roz Spencer, who had come to work for the Trust as the Housing Manager in North Kensington in 1988, was becoming increasingly concerned by the way the neighbourhood was sliding downwards again. One incident which made her realize how serious the situation had become was a conversation with one of the Trust's tenants in Powis Square. For a black man, he told Roz, it was no longer *"a good place to live"*.

The problems with the housing were accentuated by the acute level of deprivation in the area. The worst problem was the increasing use of "crack" cocaine, a drug whose lethality was only then being grasped. There were known crack houses in the area, with dealers selling drugs and large numbers of users. For many years use of drugs had been common in the area, but the use of crack was leading to much more chaotic and violent behaviour. Residents were increasingly scared by what was happening, and reluctant to challenge it for fear of reprisal.

After much discussion a group of residents resolved to take action, and attended several criminal trials to demonstrate support for police prosecutions. Their presence powerfully demonstrated the strength of local feeling. Unlike the early days, this time it was on the side of the police.

When it was first agreed to try and set up a regeneration project, there were no obvious sources of funding it, until a possibility came via the announcement by central government of the City Challenge fund. A bid was drawn up, which was supported by the Council and became one of the seven successful City Challenge schemes in London.

Sarah Harrison was appointed the Co-ordinator of the Colville Project. She had been born and grew up in North Kensington, and remembers as a teenager the excitement of the community struggles of the late 1960s, including the fight to open up Powis Square for local use. Her older brother, Nick Harrison, had reported on community events as a journalist for the Kensington Post in the late 1960s. Prior to joining the Trust she had worked for a number of years as a community development worker.

The Trust commissioned Gerard Lemos to write the history of the Colville project. He was a well-known housing consultant, with a talent for vivid descriptions and his book "Urban Village, Global City" graphically portrays what was wrong with the housing in the area as well as the wider difficulties that residents were experiencing:

"By the early 1990s the Colville neighbourhood was in urgent need of upgrading. Quite apart from the wear and tear of 15 years of use, standards of the 1960s and 1970s were no longer acceptable. The heating systems and the standards of thermal insulation were inadequate, the sound-proofing was poor and exacerbated the 'stacking' problems, where families were living in maisonettes above single people.

Crime in the home was also a problem. Burglary, particularly because of the poorly visible basement flats and the weak front doors, was a regular bane. All of this together, with the degradation of the external environment, combined to produce an alarming statistic: 35 per cent of tenants said they wanted to move." [1]

The re-improvement programme led to major works on 127 properties. Each improvement typically included repairs to the external fabric of the building, improvements to the internal layouts of the flats, renewal of mechanical and electrical services, new kitchen and bathroom fittings, installation of central heating, upgrading of thermal insulation, improved sound-proofing, and upgraded means of escape and security. In some properties new roofs, plumbing works and dry and wet rot treatment were also necessary. In all £12.9 million was spent on improving housing in the area and building new homes over three years.

One of the most successful features of the Colville Project was the shop front premises which were opened at 108 Talbot Road – or "108" as it became known - in the heart of the area. The opening of the shop was the result of a successful campaign by the Colville Area Residents Federation, for a base for the project in the Colville Area, one that would be separate from the Trust's Area office in All Saints Road.

In his book Gerard Lemos describes it as the equivalent of the village shop-cum-post-office which play such a valuable role in many rural communities. He writes:

"The development of 108 as a visible, independent centre, at arms' length from local landlords and with a brief to look at the needs of all local residents, not just for housing and not just for tenants captured the imagination of the Colville community".

It became a place to display plans for consultation and to hold meetings; to give advice on housing improvements or energy efficiency; and to discuss ideas for upgrading the local environment.

Overall responsibility for the Colville Project lay with the Colville Area Council. The membership of this included representatives of both the Notting

Hill and the Kensington Housing Trusts, the Borough Council, housing association and council tenants and the police. There was a separate Black and Minority Residents Group to ensure proper representation of their interests.

The Isokon flats

One of the most interesting and unusual developments by the Trust has been the conversion of the Isokon flats in Lawn Road, Camden. This grade I listed building was famous when it was built in 1934 for its innovative design, as an outstanding example of the Modernist school of architecture.

During its early years it was home to a group of artists, writers and poets and some of the leading names of British Modernism. Residents included Henry Moore, Barbara Hepworth, and Agatha Christie. It was the first experiment in the UK of communal high density living, intended for people who wanted a home unhampered by lots of possessions.

The name Isokon came from the building company, Isometric Unit Construction. On the ground floor was a bar, which came to be known as the Isobar, which was run by Jack Pritchard who had been the driving force behind the building of the flats.

Over the years the original residents moved out as the fashion for such small flats waned, and the building was sold to Camden Council in the 1970s. Unfortunately the housing pressures on the Council led to the density of occupation being increased, and resulted in tensions between older tenants and parents with children. The condition of the building deteriorated, and the Council was unable to find the money to carry out the comprehensive refurbishment that was needed.

Its response was to sponsor a competition for proposals to conserve and renovate the building. The Trust teamed up with the architects Avanti and won the competition. It was awarded a grant by the Housing Corporation to provide key worker accommodation. 25 studio shared ownership flats will be sold to full-time teachers working in local schools, with an option to buy between 25% to 80% of the full market value. If they move out, the flats will be re-sold to other Camden teachers.

Ten flats were sold through a local estate agent on the open market. The agents publicised an open day on a Sunday in February 2004, and all the flats were sold by the end of the afternoon. The Trust brochure for the development expressed an eloquent view of how the vision of Isokon is still relevant today:

"There is no doubt, however, that the legacy of Isokon lives on and has helped to shape our thinking, not only with regard to the built environment – many buildings in the UK were inspired by Isokon – but also in respect of how we live our

lives. Isokon is a living reminder of a simple and functional way of life that is perhaps needed today more than ever. It seems that Modernism can still provide practical solutions for the present and the future as to how we will function and survive in our increasingly crowded cities".

New developments
In addition to developments solely dependent on Social Housing Grant for subsidy, the Trust had been successful in securing funding through developers under "Section 106" agreements, where the costs of providing affordable homes were subsidized as a condition of the landowner or developer securing planning permission.

One innovative example of this was the flats built above the spectacular glass-and-steel Tesco supermarket in Warwick Road, South Kensington. To inspect the results, the scheme was visited in September 2000 by the leading architect, Richard Rogers, the local Tory MP, Michael Portillo, and members of the Mayor's Housing Commission.

Temporary housing for homeless families
From the mid 1980s there was a worrying increase in the growth of homelessness in London. The number of homeless households in temporary accommodation rose from 1,000 in 1981 to 8,000 by 1987. In west London concentrations of families in bed and breakfast hotels developed in Earls Court and Bayswater especially.

Perversely, bed and breakfast hotels are the most expensive form of temporary accommodation, and yet also the least satisfactory for homeless people. The term "hotel" is frequently highly misleading. Families can be forced to live in a single room, sharing a toilet, bathroom and cooking facilities with other residents.

In response to this increase in homelessness the Trust set up its Temporary Housing Division in 1987, and John Gregory, the Area Manager for Kensington and Chelsea, was appointed to head it. Its main activity was to lease properties that were vacant from private owners, usually on a three year term, and make them available for an agreed charge to a local authority that had large numbers of families in temporary accommodation.

The number of homes being managed by the Temporary Housing Division has grown substantially in recent years, the Division now manages 800 units in the London Borough of Newham alone, and has a separate east London office to manage them. Newham Council has more families in temporary housing than any other London borough, mainly as the result of a controversial decision by the Council in the mid 1990s to reduce dramatically the priority given to re-housing homeless families into permanent accommodation. In total, the Council has over 5,000 households in temporary housing, and some tenants face waits of five years for a permanent tenancy. Other boroughs with substantial numbers of properties include Westminster, Wandsworth, Brent, Ealing and Camden.

Over the past few years the Temporary Housing Division has been one of the fastest growing parts of the Group. In 2004 it has a staff team of 200, and is responsible for the management of over 3,000 units, across 14 London boroughs. The Division expects to take on 450 additional units of temporary accommodation in 2004/5.

Because rents for temporary housing are so much higher than in permanent housing, the annual rent income of over £50 million is now higher than the income from permanent tenancies.

The Group was one of the leaders in developing the new HAMA (Housing Associations as Managing Agents) and HALS (Housing Associations as Landlords Scheme). These were devised in response to the desire by local authorities to transfer the direct responsibility for leasing properties from the local authority to the housing association.

An association had to accept this transfer of responsibility if it wished to continue with contracts for managing temporary housing, but it increased the financial risk to the association. In particular, the dependency of almost all tenants on weekly housing benefit payments makes the association acutely vulnerable to any failure in service by the local authority housing benefits section.

Running temporary housing has been recognised by the Notting Hill Housing Group as a much needed service, but also as a high-risk activity. In the late 1990s the Temporary Housing Division ran into deficit, and was in danger of being closed down by the Board. John Gregory who had managed it during its successful expansion from 1988 to 1994 was brought back. He carried out a major re-organisation over the next two years and this brought it back to financial stability.

The Division has the high levels of staff needed to provide an intensive housing management service. The Operations Team deal with telephone calls from tenants, including responding to repairs requests, offering advice on any difficulties resulting from setting up home in an unfamiliar neighbourhood, and seeking to resolve complaints from tenants or landlords.

The Tenancy Services team are caseworkers providing welfare support to tenants, including regular visits to tenants in their homes, offering advice and guidance in dealing with the difficulties that tenants may experience as a result of being homeless and liaising with external care agencies.

The Property Services team is responsible for visiting tenants regularly to report on repairs, for monitoring performance by contractors and for ensuring that properties are returned to landlords in accordance with the terms of the leases.

Madeleine Jeffrey sees temporary housing as a "cash business" with its financial viability heavily dependent on collecting rent from residents. The Division has established a professional Debt Management Team with dedicated resources focused on the experience of managing a large stock of temporary housing. This includes the office-based sign-up of new tenants to ensure speedy receipt of housing benefit.

Most of the accommodation occupied by the tenants in temporary housing consists of self-contained street properties. For those who have been housed from bed and breakfast the quality of accommodation is hugely better. The biggest drawback for tenants living in the Trust's temporary housing is the level of rents, which average £300 a week. This is because landlords charge market rents for leasing the accommodation. The majority of tenants are on income support and claim full housing benefit. For those who have jobs, or are able to find them whilst living in temporary housing, almost all their wages are taken in paying the rent.

The other major problem is the temporary nature of the accommodation and the uncertainty over when tenants may receive an offer of permanent housing. When they move in, tenants often feel this may be only for a short time. Some do not even unpack all their belongings, because they are expecting to move almost immediately. In practice, people often stay in temporary accommodation for a year or more.

Madeleine Jeffrey feels that the "temporary housing" label can cause confusion, but she recognizes the need to distinguish it from housing in settled, secure tenancies. In some ways it is surprising that the Government continues to describe households in all forms of temporary accommodation as "homeless" in the statistics it publishes. It would be more accurate to describe them as people who have been homeless and are "waiting to be rehoused".

Their reluctance to change the language may be for fear of being accused by the tabloid press of "manipulating" the statistics. It may be one example where the Government has refused to change the way statistics are presented, even though a different definition might be more accurate as well as favourable to the Government.

Supported Housing and Care

Another area of activity in the Group which has grown since the late 1980s is the Supported Housing and Care Division (SHAC). This was formerly known as the Special Projects team, when the Trust first worked with voluntary agencies in providing housing for people with "special needs" in the 1970s.

In recent years the Division has expanded rapidly, especially in projects for people with mental health difficulties and in "extra care" for frail older people. There are four residential care homes, and two providing extra care, with two more extra care homes in development.

The new extra care developments have been planned to promote as much choice and independence as possible, including flexible care arrangements which enable residents to increase or reduce the level of support they receive.

The Division provides a range of "floating support" services to people living in independent tenancies. These are funded through the Government's Supporting People programme, through contracts with local authorities who have commissioned the service.

The Direct Support service helps tenants who need extra support to manage and maintain their tenancies. This may be due to a range of needs, including physical disability, learning difficulties, mental health problems and alcohol or drug dependency.

There is a Young People's Service for young people over 16 who are at risk. This includes care leavers, single homeless people and asylum seekers. Each young person has a Support Officer, who works with between 8 and 25 people. At present the service is provided mainly in west London, although there are plans to extend across London.

A Home Support service helps people aged 55 or over who have their own tenancy, either with the Trust or another landlord. The Temporary Accommodation service gives extra support to help tenants manage and maintain their tenancy in temporary accommodation, in addition to that provided by housing officers.

The Division has also developed a model of intensive support for tenants with a history of mental illness, which includes 24 hour, 7-day access to support for tenants who may experience serious crises which require an urgent response.

There are now 200 staff employed by the Division. Strong emphasis is placed on encouraging staff to acquire qualifications, particularly the NVQ (Non-vocational Qualification) for staff providing care services, in order to build up a team of well-trained staff.

Fundraising
Mary Harvey, a striking extrovert, who has spent most of her adult life in London and Paris since leaving the west of Ireland, has been the Head of Fundraising at the Trust for the past ten years, but first helped as a volunteer

with the visual exhibition organised to mark the Trust's 25th anniversary. When Pat White returned to work for the Trust as Director of Fundraising in 1993, she developed a new fundraising strategy and asked Mary to help her, initially for one day a week. Mary found it *"intoxicating"*, and the people at the Trust *"full of passion, commitment – and intelligence"*.

Over recent years the Trust has put fundraising income into a number of innovative projects. The Construction Training Initiative (CTI) was initiated by Simon Kaplinsky, the Trust's very talented Development Director in the early 1990s. It grew out of the recognition that there was a serious skills shortage in the building industry in west London and yet there were many disadvantaged young people who were unemployed. Simon believed that the Trust could use its "market clout" to put pressure on building contractors to give opportunities to those young people, if they committed themselves to enrolling on and completing a training course.

Mary was successful in gaining the support of the Prince's Trust, and with their backing was able to bring a number of charitable funders together. As a result £160,000 was raised over three years, which enabled the Trust to co-ordinate and support the running of the scheme. The Trust now leads a partnership of housing associations that promote the scheme, including arranging access to training courses, offering employment opportunities on building sites, and providing financial support, tools and protective clothing. It is now run by a separate team in the Trust's Training section, and has become self-financing. Initially the scheme was only open for young people between 16 and 25, but this was widened to include people up to 30, because it was found that their experiences had given them an extra maturity and determination to succeed.

The scheme has been successful in recruiting young women, who have been very under-represented in building apprenticeships and training courses. Some have come from very disadvantaged backgrounds, with few educational qualifications, or in some cases none at all. A key element has been the £25,000 hardship fund, donated by the Lyons Trust, which has made it possible to give small grants to participants with no resources except income support.

The scheme offers skills training and confidence building programmes to support young people, including young care leavers, or those who have recently been homeless. The Trust's tenant support workers also reach those who fall outside the statutory requirements of government support grants.

Mary sees one of the crucial strengths of the scheme is that it has been *"utterly practical"*, focusing on succeeding in training and getting young people into jobs. In recognition of its success it was chosen by the Prince's Trust as the example of its work that the Queen should visit to show her public support for the network of charitable projects that Prince Charles promotes.

Since the scheme was started in 1996, over 180 trainees have gained permanent employment and more than 400 have achieved a recognised qualification. Building on the knowledge gained from the CTI, the Employment Initiatives Team now offers an In2Work programme which provides confidence building programmes for unemployed tenants, hostel residents and other unemployed local people. The team uses local contacts to provide work placements, and the Trust itself has provided many work placements that have led to permanent posts.

Furniture store

For many years the Trust has had a Furniture store to help tenants with very little money who were being lured into paying high interest rates when buying furniture from unscrupulous, door-knocking profiteers. Like many of the best ideas it was simple and obvious, but represented a valuable social resource, one that made a difference to people whose lives and choices were already stretched to breaking point.

The store recently moved from being based in a former underground car park in North Kensington to a large warehouse site in Hammersmith. It is available not only to the Trust's tenants, but to those of other housing associations and local authorities by providing them with essential items of second-hand furniture. Users of the service are recommended by housing officers, social workers and others in contact with vulnerable people. Each person nominated can choose up to 10 items for their new home.

The furniture is all donated in response to advertisements placed by the Trust in the local press and the charity shops. The costs of collection, any minor repairs needed, storage and distribution are met from fundraising income, although a small, nominal charge is made to those receiving the furniture, if they can afford it.

The Notting Hill Foundation

Following a review of the fundraising activates, the Group has more recently decided to create a new charitable Foundation – the Notting Hill Foundation for London.

One of the reasons for its creation is to overcome the perception among potential donors who might look at the Trust's extensive assets and conclude that it is a wealthy organisation no longer in need of their philanthropy. What such people may fail to grasp is the continuing need for funds – to underpin creative new developments such as those discussed above.

The Foundation will have its own distinct identity as well as its own board and separate accounts. In its first 3 years the Group will endow the Foundation with a gift of £300,000. This will pay salaries of the staff who can then go out and seek to raise funds, telling would-be donors that their entire contribution will go to frontline services. It is planned that the Foundation will support regeneration projects being developed by the Trust's Neighbourhood team and also the Supported Housing and Care Division.

In describing the aims of the Foundation, Mary Harvey provided a very powerful statement of the continuing relevance of the Trust's mission, still based on the successful insights of its early years.

"When imagining what fundraising could achieve in the future I was inspired by the experience of our past, especially by the energy and zeal shown by the early pioneers of the Trust through their desire to help people in desperate need. They demonstrated a passion that cut through obstacles and 'got the job done'. Combined with the creative spirit of the time, they were able to come up with solutions that were truly innovative in their day. As a result, much of Notting Hill's work became the standard by which others measured themselves".

The work of volunteers

Chapter 3 described the work of volunteers in the early years of the Trust, when teams of volunteers came regularly on workcamps to help in renovating and decorating properties which had been acquired, as well as visiting vulnerable tenants and helping with office work.

As the Trust expanded and became more professionalised, the involvement of volunteers reduced. This changed, however, in the mid-1990s with the arrival of Alison Smith. Initially she came to the Trust as a volunteer herself, helping tenants to move into new flats, and then was encouraged by Pat White to recruit more volunteers. As a result of her success in this, she was appointed to a new post of Volunteer Co-ordinator.

She found the experience of matching volunteers with tenants needing help "brilliant", and gained a deserved reputation for her energy and enthusiasm. Volunteers took on practical tasks such as helping with gardening, decorating, shopping and obtaining goods from the furniture shop. Another role was giving support by befriending tenants on a one-to-one basis. Tenants really enjoyed the help given by people who had more time to talk with them than was possible for staff. One new development was for groups of volunteers to come from companies, combining working together in a team-building exercise whilst giving practical help to tenants of the Trust.

The largest group of volunteers work in the Trust's charity shops, where they help mostly by sorting second-hand goods and selling goods to customers. Being able to rely on so much voluntary work is critical to the profits earned by the shops, all of which are donated to the Trust. Today, volunteers still outnumber paid staff in the shops.

Alison left the Trust in 2002, and the current manager of the Volunteers team is Jo Simpson, who came to the Trust from working as the volunteer co-ordinator for a large city firm. The current number of regular volunteers is over 100.

The section has a scheme for assessing the value of the contribution, by quantifying the value of an hour's activity, based on the estimated market pay for that type of work. By this yardstick this volunteers contributed £200,000 in 2003.

One volunteer who worked with the Trust in the very early days has recently offered to act as a mentor to motivate and sustain local residents who have been looking for work for a long time. A number of staff members are also volunteering, by joining a reading project in a local school.

The volunteers team is currently exploring the possibility of a new initiative involving residents on the Dalgarno estates in North Kensington to set up a "time bank", where tenants will do voluntary work for other tenants, with a time value given to each job which entitles those volunteering to receive help in return. As in regeneration projects all over the country, it has demonstrated repeatedly that participation in such community endeavours gives a sense of ownership which is vital to individual as well as collective well-being, nurturing an active and healthy citizenship where it had been allowed to wither.

---

1. *Urban Village, Global City, Gerard Lemos, Lemos and Crane, 1998.*

Chapter 13

LOOKING FORWARD

Peter Redman was the Chief Executive from 1993 to 2003, a period when the Trust was a leading recipient of Housing Corporation grant, to provide both rented and shared ownership housing. He had a strong belief in the importance of building tenanted homes of good quality, and that low standards were not acceptable. This perspective was also reflected in the importance he gave to the programme for re-investing in the Trust's existing housing stock.

Pete wanted the Group to be provide a range of housing "products", including affordable homes for the growing number of households in London who could not afford to buy their home outright, even where two households were earning. He expounded robust views on the importance of the Trust not owning estates occupied only by poor people and thus a belief in socially mixed communities. He was an advocate of giving people greater choice over the homes they lived in, whilst recognizing that more choice for some often meant less for others.

For the Group these plans opened up exciting development opportunities. The Board considered whether it should seek to expand in the Thames Gateway area, but decided to continue its policy of only developing new homes in west London, building on its existing community base.

Peter Redman also played a leading role in the London Housing Federation, which he chaired for four years. When the National Housing Federation embarked on a major project to review its public identity, he was one of the active participants in the subsequent debate, and chaired one of the working groups set up to develop the proposals.

At its Annual conference in September 2002 the NHF launched its "In Business for Neighbourhoods" brand, urging all members of the Federation to endorse it, and adopt it for their own association. The market research commissioned by the Federation found that many people saw associations as housing only low-income tenants. Associations were also believed to do too little to counter anti-social behaviour.

The key message of "In Business for Neighbourhoods" fitted in comfortably with the strategic approach to neighbourhoods and the emphasis on community development which the Group had promoted over a number of years, through projects such as the Colville Project, the Dalgarno Project, and the proposals for Grahame Park. These could be seen as an exemplar of the NHF policy that all housing associations should see themselves not simply as providers of bricks and mortar, but as promoters of sustainable neighbourhoods.

The mission statement commits associations to tackle anti-social behaviour, as a crucial ingredient in the development of communities where people positively want to live. What it does not really address, however, is what may happen to people excluded or evicted from those communities. This is one of the key issues for associations like the Notting Hill Housing Trust, which has always been committed to reaching out to the most disadvantaged.

Central government too had been slow to address the problem of anti-social behaviour and as the new century got underway Tony Blair's administration found themselves grappling, not always successfully, with a variety of attempts – including the option of obtaining an anti-social behaviour order (ASBO) – to curb unruly families without punishing the innocent or merely shifting a problem elsewhere.

A Board member who became active working in the Trust in early 1994 is Penny Hutton. She had run a large cosmetics company and worked abroad in the Far East for eight years. On her return she moved back to Notting Hill, where she had lived previously. She was surprised at the extent of visible homelessness in London, and shocked by a conversation she had one day with an elderly woman who was sleeping rough at Victoria Station.

The next morning a fundraising appeal from the Trust dropped through her front door. She telephoned to ask if there were ways she might help, and spoke to Pat White, who suggested she should talk with Peter Redman. After having a meeting with him she took on a role in re-integrating the charity shops into the Group and making them more profitable. For two years she chaired the Shops Board, and was then asked to become a member of the Group Board.

When she joined the Board, she found it very large and often cumbersome, partly through its conscious effort to be inclusive of different interests. There were a number of sub-committees, and these were taking a lot of time both for Board members and senior executives.

As a result of concerns about the way the Board was operating, an appraisal was carried out which resulted in a reduction in its membership. Instead of having sub-Committees a new system was introduced whereby "lead members" took responsibility for different areas of activity.

After six years in office Lionel Morrison decided to stand down as Chair. He had been suffering from poor health and felt he should step aside. As a result it was decided to look for a successor with a higher public profile, accustomed to public controversy as well as possessing the range of skills needed to chair what had now become a large and complex social business. The Board was delighted when, in 1999, Lord Sawyer agreed to take on this role. He had been a leading public sector trade unionist in what is now UNISON before being appointed the General Secretary of the Labour Party and leading it through a critical period of change during Neil Kinnock's leadership. He then went on to become an active member of the House of Lords.

After carrying through the changes to the Board's operating practices, the Group embarked on a major reassessment of how well it provided services to its existing tenants and lessees. It was becoming aware that it needed both to improve the responsiveness and the cost effectiveness of its housing services. This was prompted by a growing awareness of criticism by tenants and lessees about some of the services.

A tenant survey carried out in 1997 showed that 74% of tenants were satisfied with their home. A similar proportion also thought the Trust to be a good landlord, which was lower than the previous survey (81%). Only 7% thought it was a poor landlord, rising to 30% amongst those who were dissatisfied with their home. While these overall satisfaction levels were high, some findings about services tenants received from the Trust were a cause for concern:

- When they sought advice or assistance on the telephone, over a third of tenants said the person they spoke to could not deal with the problem.
- Only half found it easy to contact the right person.
- Almost one fifth found staff unhelpful.

To decide what changes were needed, 550 staff and 50 voluntary committee members took part in a special programme of team sessions seeking to find out what tenants and lessees wanted. This was called the "Customer First" programme. In addition, a firm of external consultants, Life Skills International, was appointed to work with staff to help them develop a more user focused approach. Not for the first time a debate within the Trust both reflected and anticipated wider trends in society which would increasingly refocus public services like schools and the NHS on the needs of the "customer" in a consumer society. It was seen as a means of making a large social organisation – a housing association or a hospital – both more responsive and more efficient.

Following on from this programme the Board decided to set up the "Passionate About Customer Services" project, with the brief to draw up detailed proposals for new arrangements. This was led by Steve Coleman, who transferred from being Director of Home Ownership.

Within the Group there was a view that traditional arrangements for a locally based housing management service might no longer be appropriate and that a more centralised structure, one organised around key functions, might prove more effective.

From the experience of other organisations, including a number of larger housing associations, a central "customer service" structure was seen as offering a proven solution. The basic idea was that a call centre with highly trained staff would deal with the majority of queries, and that this would be backed up by functional teams to do whatever might be needed as a result.

Another important recommendation was to set up a single, central management team for both leasehold and rented housing, on the grounds that there was no reason why the Trust should not offer the same professional service to customers regardless of their tenure.

The most controversial issue arising from the "Passionate About Customer Services" review was the proposal to close the Area offices. The Trust had devolved management to local offices for over thirty years. Some staff and Area Committee members feared that the change would diminish vital contact between tenants and housing management staff, and were sceptical about the claims made for the new centralised service. The local authorities were also critical of the proposals, which they saw as weakening the Trust's commitment to local accountability.

Since leaving All Saints Road in the heart of Notting Hill, the Trust's head office had initially been in Paddenswick Road, Hammersmith, later at Grove House in Hammersmith Grove, a mile to the east. As such the main offices are close to Hammersmith Broadway, so that tenants and leaseholders in the Hammersmith and Fulham area are still able to come to a local office. Understandably, given the history of the Trust (indeed its very name!) the strongest opposition was to the closure of the North Kensington Area office in All Saints Road where it had been for over 30 years.

A response to these critics is that they are looking back with nostalgia to something which no longer exists. Overall the Trust's stock is more widely spread and less geographically concentrated than it used to be. The case for a locally based area office, within walking distance for tenants, many without easy access to any form of telephone in those early days, may be much weaker than it was thirty years ago.

There are undoubtedly still pockets of real poverty and deprivation in North Kensington, but there are few private landlords renting to low income tenants. Most properties being let or sold can only be afforded by high income earners. The activities of the Council and housing associations have been successful in preserving a substantial stock of good quality rented homes which enable lower income people to live in the area, but newcomers are almost exclusively the rich. An unpredicted aspect of the Trust's legacy has been social diversity in what has become a wealthy neighbourhood. It is precisely that goal it seeks to foster, albeit at a more modest level, in neighbourhoods that are unlikely to attract Hollywood stars – either on camera or as residents.

An alternative method of keeping a local presence where there is a high concentration of tenants is through neighbourhood offices, such as in the Colville area, the Dalgarno estates and at Windmill Park.

After much debate, the Board decided to implement the proposals for a central customer service, with four main elements:

a) 24 Customer Service Officers who would focus on answering enquiries and provide a range of services. Their task would be to process all initial repair requests and ring customers to get feedback on the services. They would also be a central point of contact for "customers", with the aim of answering 80% of all calls on the spot. The Customer Service Team (CST) would run the switchboard and reception centrally from Grove House.

b) 18 Neighbourhood Officers would become the named contact for customers, focusing on and regularly inspecting the estates and street properties; setting and managing the service contacts; and providing a moving-in visit for all new customers.

c) 11 Casework Officers would work with individual customers to resolve complex tenure issues like anti-social behaviour or domestic violence. The Casework officers would:

• Focus on pro-active solutions to these issues by working with external agencies.

• Take responsibility for a specific geographical "patch" where they had expert local knowledge.

• Provide expert office hours telephone support for the CST.

d) 7 Patrol Officers would provide an out of hours "professional witness and intervention service". This is seen as a visible sign of commitment by the Trust to pro-active property management, to complement the work of the Neighbourhood and Casework Officers.

One of those who was against the centralisation of services was Annabel Louvros. After being housed by the Trust she became active in her local Tenants' Association and was then voted on to the Area Committee. She was the Acting Chair when the proposals for closing the North Kensington Area office in All Saints Road were put forward. She says:

"I was fiercely, fiercely against the closure of the Area office. I personally feel that the Trust's effectiveness was undermined by being centralised. North Kensington was the seedcorn of the Trust and closing the office was terribly symbolical".

Sue Black was a member of the senior management team who also believed that closing the Area offices was a mistake. Sue had worked for the Trust over almost thirty years and felt that the local base in North Kensington was crucial to the organisation's identity. Nevertheless, the senior management team took a majority decision which she then supported.

Sue felt exhausted by being increasingly out of step and resigned her post of Group Director of Development and New Business in January 2001, and left in July that year. She remains very committed to the organisation despite these later differences and in March 2004, she joined the Notting Hill Foundation as a Board member.

The change also affected the relationship with some of the key local authorities, which saw the change as downgrading the importance of the Trust's relationship with their borough. This concern was compounded by the changed management structures, which removed Area Directors who had been the main link between the Trust and the local authorities.

When the new arrangements were introduced there was a significant increase in repair requests. As elsewhere in the field of public service reform this seemingly perverse consequence was actually a sign of success, attributed to customers being able to get repairs carried out more easily. One inevitable consequence was that, as the number of orders increased, so the budget was overspent.

Steve Coleman was responsible for the overall management of the new arrangements, as the Director of Customer Services. When he left the Group in 2003 John Gregory replaced him as the Acting Director. He has been in a very good position to assess the impact of the Customer Services re-organisation. While acknowledging the advantages of a central service, the biggest mistake in John's view proved to be the decision to bring both tenants and lessees into the same teams. In his experience the nature of the service they want and expect are significantly different.

2003 was a difficult year for the Trust. The major reorganisation needed to launch the call centre was followed by a further decline in housing management performance. It has been a common experience for housing associations which have transferred to a call centre structure that initially performance falls. But it came at a bad time for the Group.

When the Audit Commission made its first full inspection of the Trust, its auditors were critical of a number of aspects of performance. They concluded that the governance arrangements of the Group needed review and that:

"There is scope for considerable improvement in lettings, repairs and maintenance, and especially with regard to the responsive repairs service, asset management and payments to contractors.

Performance in collecting rents and service charges has not yet responded to the strategic changes which have been put in place, and there is still scope for improvement".

The Audit Commission was also critical of the Group's governance arrangements, saying *"the Board needs to take further action to ensure capable leadership of the organisation".*

As in the drive to improve the efficiency and effectiveness of schools and hospitals the star rating system had by now reached the world of housing associations. The Audit Commission's overall rating gave the Group only one star (out of a maximum of three) under the heading which noted that there was *"scope for improvement, but that it is raising standards".*

The tough verdict was given considerable publicity in the housing press, coming so soon after critical reports on several other leading associations. One unfortunate result was that the Trust was not included among the 71 major associations given the new "partnership" status by the Housing Corporation, with development allocations for the two year period from 2004 - 2006. After decades at the cutting edge of innovation and reform that was a bitter pill to swallow.

With hindsight Penny Hutton believes that the Group was seen as arrogant and self-righteous by its critics. It had been a market leader, but had now fallen behind in some areas of performance. Change would be needed if the Trust was to restore its standing.

After discussing his position with the Board, Peter Redman announced his resignation, and left the Trust in September 2003. He had led the Group as Chief Executive for ten years through major changes in the external environment and a range of successful developments by the Group. These included the growth of low cost home ownership, the expansion of supported housing and of temporary accommodation, a range of mixed tenure housing schemes and the development of the strategy for successful neighbourhoods.

The Board appointed Ingrid Reynolds, the Director of Property and New Business, as the Acting Chief Executive. She had worked for the previous ten years as Development Director of the Acton Housing Association, and prior to that worked for Circle 33 Housing Trust.

By the early months of 2004 considerable progress was being made in overcoming the problems. The Housing Corporation gave the Group substantial capital allocations for new development in 2004/5 and 2005/6. The allocation for the second year was the highest in the country for an association outside the "partnership" associations.

Ingrid Reynolds led the Executive Management Team in preparing a new Business Plan for 2004 to 2008, which sets out a clear strategy for the next four years. This starts with a new vision statement:

"We want to be the housing association of choice in London: shaping communities that people feel proud to live in".

It then sets out four key objectives:

* *"Deliver the best quality landlord service.*
* *Regain our position as a respected, innovative and growing association in London, with the target of building 1,000 new homes a year by 2006/7.*
* *By the end of the plan significantly increase the number of homes owned or managed for new customers.*
* *Build a focused and sustainable business through the commercial management of our activities and adopt a realistic approach to the management of risk".*

Central to the revised strategy is the aim of building on the Group's reputation for having strong roots in local communities, and working to promote inclusive and sustainable neighbourhoods.

The Trust made its reputation working with the local community in North Kensington, and then extended this in Hammersmith and to developments in other west London boroughs. The regeneration projects in Colville, Earls Court and new estates such as the Rootes development have built on this record. With these it has developed a vision for neighbourhoods, which is at the heart of its plans for the future.

In May 2004 Kate Davies was appointed as the new Chief Executive. She was the Chief Executive of Servite Houses, with extensive experience in the social housing sector, including as the Director of Housing at Brighton and Hove Council.

Board members believe that Kate Davies has the range of qualities which the Group seeks from its new Chief Executive. As Penny Hutton puts it *"Kate is proven and respected, and also charismatic and inspirational. She is an entrepreneur who is pragmatic. She believes that our customers should have the opportunity to be involved in whatever way they want".*

After discussion with members of the Board, the senior management team and the Housing Corporation, Kate came to the conclusion that the most urgent priority was to make the changes which would enable the Group to be given a "green light" by the Housing Corporation for its governance arrangements – the indication it now uses to show it is satisfied.

The Board had already commissioned Julian Ashby from the consultants HACAS Chapman Hendy to advise them on what changes might be required in the role and composition of the Board. He has been a managing partner of HACAS since it was formed thirty years ago, and has unrivalled experience in advising housing associations on their governance arrangements.

Kate presented proposals for a new governance structure for the Group to a special Board meeting in June 2004. These set out the skills needed by its members, among them those of large scale business and financial management, property development, housing management, vision and entrepreneurial skills, customer perspective and local knowledge and connections. It proposed that there should be two tenant members and one staff member on the Board, *"as a potent symbol of the partnership which exists between customers, staff and the Board"* and recognising the *"valued perspective"* that tenant Board members bring.

The paper also recommended that the Group should adopt the National Housing Federation Code requirements in full. Board members should be appointed for three year terms of office. The maximum period of Board service should be 9 years.

The crucial and painful conclusion was that the current Board did not possess some of the core skills necessary. It was proposed, therefore, that the entire Board should "stand down". This was seen as an opportunity for "the Board to demonstrate its own leadership and commitment to excellence", and a recognition that "the regulator (the Housing Corporation) is looking for a grand gesture and a commitment to a fresh start".

The Board decided unanimously to approve the proposals in the paper. All members therefore offered their resignation, so that a recruitment process could start immediately, with the aim of ensuring that a new board would include members with the full range of skills needed to face new challenges in an increasingly complex social and political environment.

Among those standing down was Tom Sawyer, who had always made it known that he would only serve as chair for five years. An ad hoc committee of outgoing board members and senior Trust executives interviewed prospective successors. In mid-2004 it decided to appoint Gerard Lemos, a social entrepreneur with a strong housing background and long professional connections with the Trust, as its new chairman.

The Trust has had a succession of very different chairmen, including a senior judge, a barrister, a black journalist and, in Tom Sawyer, a trade unionist from the North East. In appointing Gerard, an outgoing Indian Catholic, it took another turn. A formidable networker, consultant and writer on social policy, he is also a deputy chair of the British Council and, until his appointment to the chair at Notting Hill, was a board member at the Audit Commission – the very body whose critique had prompted widespread change at the Trust.

These changes had constituted a series of difficult decisions for the board and management of the Trust. The Board's collective resignation was the climax of a period of rapid, often-unsettling change. But in accepting its own share of responsibility for acknowledged failures the Board had acted boldly and for the wider public good – as it had done so often in the past.

Chapter 14

CONCLUSIONS

The history of the Notting Hill Housing Trust contains many fascinating and memorable events, which have been described in the previous chapters. This chapter draws some conclusions from the Trust's work which may be relevant for the future.

Developing social mixed communities

The Trust's most important achievement has clearly been in providing 18,000 affordable homes, but another significant achievement has been its role in developing socially mixed communities.

When the Trust began it was simply buying properties to house desperately overcrowded families, with no conscious aim of promoting socially balanced, mixed tenure communities. However, as the number of homes owned by the Trust grew, the mix of tenures became an important feature of the neighbourhoods where the Trust was active.

Compared to the single tenure, Council-owned, housing estates, what was different about those neighbourhoods was the way in which owner-occupied, privately rented and housing association properties quietly co-existed in almost every street, usually without being visible to a stranger's eye, let alone commented upon. In an age of growing social polarisation this in itself was a substantial achievement.

In these areas the Trust was not only providing homes for rent. An important form of housing it pioneered was the development of low cost home ownership, through the plans for "community leasehold". Again the impetus for this came from the recognition of a gap in the housing provision, the lack of affordable housing for people on moderate incomes.

The Conservative Government's support for shared ownership was primarily ideological. It was seen as a means of extending the opportunity of home ownership to those who could not afford to buy outright. For the Trust the motive was in sustaining socially balanced communities, where people on low, middle and higher incomes were all able to live.

The Trust was also one of the first housing associations to develop "special needs" accommodation, developing projects in partnership with specialist voluntary agencies. Over the years this provision for people with mental health needs, physical and mental disabilities, women escaping domestic violence, and people vulnerable for other reasons, has expanded into a major strand of housing association activity. Today the Care and Supported Housing Division is an integral part of the Notting Hill Housing Group, with well-trained staff providing high quality services.

Monolithic system-built housing estates became frequent objects of attack. Yet curiously few voices on either side of the polarised debate spoke out to praise the successes of housing improvement programmes, especially in inner city areas, where local councils, private owners and housing associations had worked together in renovating older homes and preserving existing communities. Years before public/private sector partnerships became the fashion, Housing Action Areas were a demonstration of how they could work.

This feature of the Trust's work should not be seen only as an interesting feature of its history. The promotion of socially mixed communities has now emerged as a key goal of the Government's housing policy, and also of the Mayor's London Housing Strategy. Currently it is applied only to new developments, but it could be applied to the existing housing stock.

For example, local authorities could sell flats on their housing estates in order to buy street properties, in order to reduce the concentration of rented properties and widen the choice of lettings. There is an urgent need to provide permanent homes for the huge number of homeless families in temporary accommodation, which could be achieved by buying those, or similar, street properties rather than paying out huge market rents every year.

Successful community action

For anyone who wants to understand better how social change can be influenced in local communities the experiences in Notting Hill in the 1960s and 70s are a rich source of evidence.

Chapter 5 "A Cauldron of Community Activity" described the huge community campaign which led to a transformation in housing policy. The change that took place was the outcome of two different processes. One was the intense pressure from the sustained campaigning of local community organisations, combined with the invaluable credibility the Trust gained from its successful record of housing renewal and the strong consensus developed on alternative policy solutions. The other was the shift of power within the dominant political agency, the Borough Council. This enabled the new Leader to embrace a very different approach, which combined a new set of housing policies and a new political strategy towards the long neglected poorer section of the borough.

The lessons are not primarily from individual events or tactics. Some activities were undoubtedly important and can be replicated in a similar form. The 1967 Housing Survey provided irrefutable evidence of the urgent need for action. The People's Association relentlessly organised and supported protest activities, publicised every week by the People's News and local newspapers. The Clinch study of the Colville/Tavistock area played a crucial role in demonstrating that the existing policy would not halt the erosion of affordable homes.

What was most important, however, for achieving change was the unity over policy goals and the collective impact generated through many different forms and styles of lobbying.

Some activities, such as the "lock-in", were highly controversial. They were celebrated by at least some participants as huge successes but by critics as dangerously counter-productive. Yet the opponents of change were not able to isolate individuals or organisations. There was no overall campaign structure, no formal coalition, but there was a web of interlocking relationships, some formal but probably even more important were those that were informal.

The significance of what was achieved does not lie only in the change of political direction and social policies. As argued in Chapter 6, what was achieved was the empowerment of the community. The distribution of power in North Kensington was still unequal, poorer residents still enjoyed little control over most aspects of their lives. Yet the community no longer experienced the depth of powerlessness which had been such a defining feature of life in Notting Hill's earlier years.

Underpinning these wider changes was the work of the housing associations. Without secure homes for low income people to live in all the other community gains would have lost their value. As has happened with many urban renewal projects all over the world, low income residents would have been displaced by affluent newcomers

In striking contrast, the housing associations in North Kensington had snatched properties from under the noses of property developers, bought homes in competition with private bidders and turned dilapidated houses into self-contained flats. In the words of a notable People's News article, in the battle to achieve this, the Notting Hill Housing Trust were *"on our side"*.

Regenerating older neighbourhoods
The Trust played a key role in a significant number of HAAs, declared in neighbourhoods with high levels of multi-occupation and overcrowding, where many properties were suffering from disrepair and lacking modern

amenities. By the end of the five year life of the HAAs more than 90% of the housing had been improved to a satisfactory standard.

The HAA programme should have been recognised as a model of successful, neighbourhood-based housing renewal. Sadly, its achievements were largely ignored. The Conservative Government's housing priority in the 1980s was to promote home ownership. The Labour Party and local authorities were pre-occupied in their defensive struggle to protect municipal housing.

The approach of the HAAs could be effective today in areas of poor quality, privately owned housing, working closely with the local community, combining private resources with public investment and preserving socially balanced communities through diversity of tenure.

Influencing national events

The Trust also played a key role in national events, showing that local organisations can have a powerful influence on a wider stage.

Through Bruce Kenrick, the Trust played the leading role in setting up the very dynamic campaign for the homeless, Shelter. It was launched with massive national publicity in December 1966 and developed into the major national charity campaigning on behalf of homeless and badly housed people and raising public awareness by its high profile campaigning. Forty years on it is the recognised national voice for homeless and badly housed people, with 700 staff and an annual income of over £30 million a year.

The Trust also became an acknowledged leader of the new generation of charitable housing associations, rehabilitating older properties in inner city areas of housing stress. And it was a key player in persuading successive Governments to create a new funding regime, which would pave the way for a massive expansion of housing association activity.

Working with private lenders

The 1988 Housing Act marked a watershed in Government policy towards housing associations. Loans had to be sought from private lenders, grant rates were cut, associations had to compete for funding.

The new arrangements faced associations with a complex array of choices, opportunities and challenges. Some decided that the priority for the future was to "chase the funding", doing whatever maximized the prospects for pleasing the statutory and private funders, whether that was raising rents, cutting development costs or embracing new tenure options. Such a strategy may have yielded short term gains for the associations which embraced it, but too often it has not led to affordable homes of good standard being nurtured in sustainable communities.

In recent years many associations have defined themselves as businesses. Tenants and lessees are called "customers". The rationale for this language is that associations must project themselves as efficient, professional and credible with private funders and focused on the expectations of those who use their services.

The danger is that associations may appear no different from any private sector organisation, where the primary motive is profit. Board members and staff may come to believe that the altruistic motives which drew them into work with housing associations are no longer relevant in the new style Registered Social Landlords, as they became designated by the 1996 Housing Act. Where that has happened it is a sad mistake. The long term winners are likely be those who root their strategies and business plans in understanding not only housing but also social and economic needs, and then plan cost-effective and innovative ways of meeting them.

The Notting Hill Housing Group has adopted the terminology of being a business. It is clear, however, that it is a *social* business, where the objectives remain the same as when the Trust was launched in 1963. The distinction was well expressed by the French politician who said that he wanted to live "in a market economy, but not a market society".

There are a range of ways in which the Trust now compares favourably with what it did in the early years. For example, although the Trust was exceptional in having a welfare worker, and then a qualified social worker, from early in its life, the support given to vulnerable tenants was modest compared to the services the current Housing Care and Support team provide, for example the access to 24 hour support for tenants living at home with mental health problems. The Colville Project and stock reinvestment programme improved the Trust's properties to a much higher standard than that achieved in the early conversions and offered not just housing, but also a range of services and activities for the local community.

Building new estates

Over the past 15 years the Trust has had to learn new skills for managing housing estates with large numbers of non-earning and vulnerable tenants. In response it has developed policies for new forms of estate design, the integration of different tenures, applying different lettings policies and employing community development workers.

For example on the Rootes estate in North Kensington, the Trust worked with its partners to develop a vision for the neighbourhood, with home ownership and rented homes, a range of community facilities and projects to help residents train for employment.

The plans for the Grahame Park estate show how a monolithic, one tenure council estate will be replaced by a mixed tenure development, with homes in different tenures "pepper-potted" across the estate. Because the two housing associations will own the land, they will be able to ensure that their vision for the new neighbourhood is reflected on the ground.

Key personalities

The pages of this book are filled with descriptions of those who have played an important role in the Trust's development. Trying to name them all would be an impossible task.

However, there are two people who stand out. The first was Bruce Kenrick, the key figure in the formation of the Trust and the setting up of Shelter. He only played an active role in the Trust for four years, from 1963 to 1967. His involvement in Shelter spanned a still shorter period, from the initial idea of a new organisation in 1965 until 1967.

Since it is now so long since he was active, few people now in the voluntary housing movement know him personally. Even fewer are aware of the significance of his achievements. Most people know only of the role which Des Wilson played in Shelter as the campaign's charismatic first Director. Few know that it was Bruce Kenrick who conceived the idea for Shelter, planned the sort of organisation it should be and led the negotiations to secure the support of the key national organisations. In Eammon Casey's words: *"There is no doubt that Bruce Kenrick created Shelter, and without him it would not have existed"*.

Bruce played a decisive role in the formation of two organisations, which have both made an enormous impact on the development of housing provision and responses to homelessness over the last forty years. It is sad that his health problems have prevented him being able to lead an active working life. For the past 20 years he has lived alone on the Island of Iona, and is now almost completely blind.

The other remarkable person was John Coward. He came as the Housing Manager in 1965 and immediately took control of the diverse development, management and financial responsibilities of the fledgling, fast-growing association. His professional skills, financial acumen and management abilities, combined with steady but unerring judgement were crucial to the successful growth of the Trust. They were underpinned by what proved to be this mild, bespectacled official's understated ability to gain and sustain the confidence of a wide range of interest groups, many of them mutually antagonistic.

In addition to its local preoccupations, the Notting Hill Housing Trust played a leading role in influencing national housing policies. Bruce Kenrick's flair for publicity gave the Trust a higher profile than other housing associations. John Coward's experience and professionalism gave the Trust a leading role in the advocacy and lobbying activity.

Richard Best believes that:

"John Coward was at the centre of the transformation of policies towards housing associations. His success lay not in charismatic leadership from the front, which is time-limited, but in consensus building – between the different generations of housing organisations, as well as within the new breed - an inspiration through action. He was the right person at the right time to win the confidence of policy-makers and practitioners alike".

In an article published when John Coward retired in 1986, Richard Best wrote:

"His career in the housing association movement may have had a greater impact than any other single individual's during this period. Consistently he identified key housing needs, saw that the necessary legislation and procedures moved into place to achieve them, and then pursued them vigorously himself. By showing the way, he helped things happen for an enormous number of associations".

Others who worked closely with him echo those sentiments. Anthony Taussig speaks of *"his genius for motivating people…the way he always treated everyone with respect".* Ken Bartlett acknowledges the immense debt that he personally owes John for the advice, support and sharing of ideas in the many years they worked closely together.

It is important also to recognize the contribution of other people who have played a leading role in the work of the Trust. For 20 years Sir Roger Ormrod combined his work as an eminent judge, with being a wise, rock-like Chair of the Trust. Sidney Miller, the Director of the Family Service Unit in North Kensington, was a tireless committee member, working to ensure that the Trust helped people in the greatest need, yet also constantly stressing that vulnerable tenants need support in order to retain their homes. He was aptly described as the "moral voice" of the Trust.

Anthony Taussig was the donor who gave Bruce Kenrick the money which paid for the Trust's first national fundraising advertisement. He was a committee member since 1968, until resigning in 2004 in order to enable the Group to implement new governance arrangements. He was Chair from 1988 until 1993. He has been a member and chair of Area Committees, and has chaired the Group's home ownership and commercial subsidiaries. His commitment to the Trust has been unmatched, and he has shown constant vigilance in assessing risks and protecting the interests of the Group.

Among the staff, committee and volunteers there have been countless examples of loyalty and dedication well beyond any reasonable call of duty.

And, of course, all those Trust tenant activists who discovered the spark of leadership within themselves.

Improbable players like Sir Malby Crofton, the reforming baronet who ran Kensington and Chelsea Council at a critical juncture, deserve their share of credit too. So do grassroots radicals like John and Jan O'Malley who gave Sir Malby - and John Coward - a very hard time.

A remarkable organisation

Over the past forty years there have been huge changes in the way that the Trust has worked. It began very much as a "loner", working on its own to provide homes. From the early 1970s this changed as it started to work more closely with community groups and to develop a partnership with the Borough Council. Over the following years the range of partnerships widened, with voluntary agencies in providing supported housing, with local authorities and with the Housing Corporation.

From the 1980s onwards, however, the Trust found itself acting more often as an agent, especially of central Government as it developed new programmes. So the Conservative Government looked to Addison as one of the leading associations for promoting low cost home ownership. More recently, with the emergence of the Communities Plan, the Labour Government has been wanting housing associations to provide a much expanded programme of affordable new homes in the south east. The Housing Corporation seems to see them primarily as "delivery agents".

A crucial question for the Notting Hill Housing Group, of which the Trust remains the anchor, is how it sees its role. There are many points at which its own priorities coincide with the Government's agenda – and that of the Housing Corporation - such as increasing the provision of affordable housing for key public sector workers squeezed by the overheated London property market and in doing so to create socially mixed, sustainable communities. There are others points of policy direction where there are different views, and the Group feels it has little option but to comply with the expectations of the Housing Corporation.

Yet the Group is an independent organisation. It can argue and negotiate. It can take initiatives, with other partners where appropriate, which do not depend on funding from central government, or even any public money. It can help to shape a new agenda and develop new ways of providing homes and promoting inclusive, vibrant new communities. If the past is a guide, central government eventually catches up. Independence, material and intellectual, remains vital.

The success of the community campaign in North Kensington in the early 1970s came from a belief that the Council's housing policies could be changed, in order to tackle the problems of run-down, older homes and to stop tenants being evicted by ruthless developers. The outcome was a partnership where the Trust worked with an initially reluctant local Council and community organisations in a groundbreaking programme of housing renewal.

Housing needs now are very different from those when the Trust started. There has been real success especially in reducing the number of tenants living in poor quality, multi-occupied and overcrowded properties. Now there are different problems and an urgent need for new solutions. For example, there is an urgent need to help tenants living in severely overcrowded council or housing association flats, which might be achieved by enabling tenants living in under-occupied flats to choose their own flat in the country and move out.

In writing this book I have been conscious of a danger that an account of the extraordinary achievements of the early years of the Trust could glamorise the past and unwittingly make the present seem to be a disappointing anti-climax. The difficulties experienced by the Group in the recent past may accentuate this danger, but unless history is recorded it is easily forgotten.

The history of social housing is not as glamorous as that of high politics and the "isms" which obsess ambitious politicians and media commentators alike. Yet having a secure and decent home is one of the essential foundations of a fulfilled life. As former President Bill Clinton sometimes puts it, it is one of the ingredients which allows more people to have "a good story" to tell. The Notting Hill Housing Trust has helped thousands of tenants, who might otherwise have struggled to survive, to have good stories instead.

My own view is that the vision and passion which fired those who launched the Trust in the early 1960s is still there today. I believe that the best of what is being done by the Group today in building new socially mixed and inclusive communities and regenerating deprived neighbourhoods is as inspiring as the work that was done to bring new hope to disadvantaged communities in the 1960s. It is still desperately needed by the people who will benefit. In some ways achieving this is more difficult, especially because of the wider range of "stakeholders" who must be satisfied, the demanding performance targets set by government, and the scrutiny of external regulators.

What has been remarkable in researching this book is consistently finding the strength of commitment of those who have worked with the Trust. Repeatedly it has been described in phrases such as *"there was always a buzz"*, *"a wonderful place to work"*, *"fantastic people to work with"*, and time and again, *"the best job I have ever had"*. Those have come from people working with the

Trust now and from every stage in its history. Tenants too, the people for whom the Trust was established in the first place, speak with quiet satisfaction of how their lives were changed. Most of the time.

This book records the history of one of the inner city based associations, set up in a critical period in the 1960s. From that family first housed in 1964, the Trust has grown to be landlord to 50,000 people. At its heart this is a story of commitment to marginalized people which has inspired staff, volunteers and committee members for the past forty years. They are at the very core of what has made the Trust not just a good organisation, but at its best a *great* one.

Appendix

NOTTING HILL HOUSING GROUP MILESTONES

Date	Milestone	National Context
1963	• First committee meeting held on 18 December, chaired by Rev. Bruce Kenrick	
1964	• 5 houses purchased • First tenants housed • £58k received in donations (= over £500k at 2003 prices)	• General Election, Labour Government elected
1965	• John Coward appointed as Housing Manager • 17 houses bought • Sir Milner Holland speaks at Trust AGM	• Report of Milner Holland Inquiry into Housing in Greater London
1966	• Property conversions by direct labour • Decorations by volunteer work parties • National fundraising ceased when Bruce Kenrick founded Shelter • Rent rebate scheme for Trust tenants	• November:"Cathy Come Home" shown on TV • 1st December, launch of Shelter, with Bruce Kenrick as the Chair
1967	• 100th house opened in St Luke's Road • Trust started buying occupied properties • 50% nomination rights given to GLC in exchange for subsidy	• New clause put in Housing Bill, following Bruce Kenrick's dinner with the Minister, Anthony Greenwood

- Waiting list closed to families with more than 1 child
- 100 volunteers came to Notting Hill for Summer Project and housing survey

1968
- Hon Mr Justice Ormrod became Chair
- 48 Collingbourne Road given to Trust
- 452 days by volunteer work parties

1969
- New offices and flats at All Saints House opened by Princess Margaret
- Notting Hill Housing Service published report of Housing Survey
- First qualified Social Worker and Volunteers Organiser appointed
- Royal Borough of Kensington and Chelsea (RBKC) invited Trust to work on large-scale programme of acquisition and renewal in North Kensington
- Detailed evidence sent to Cohen Committee re role for HA's

1970
- 100 houses bought in year for first time
- Area office opened in Shepherd's Bush
- Tenant representatives to sit on Tenants & Welfare Sub-Committee
- Deficit finance scheme with RBKC
- LB Ealing handed 20 short-life houses to Trust
- 2 show houses opened by Anthony Greenwood, the Housing Minister

1971
- United Housing Association Trust (UHAT) established
- Colville/Tavistock Study launched to examine policies for area improvement.

- White paper "Old Houses into New Homes", which led to 1969 Housing Act and improvement grants
- New Housing Act, with boost for improvement grants
- Housing Associations (HA's) now being seen as third choice for those seeking housing

- General Election: Conservative Government elected

1972	• First tenants association formed • Fires and squatting problems • First charity shop opened in Putney • First commercial portfolio acquired	• Housing Finance Act, created "Fair rents" for housing associations tenants and new system of rent allowances
1973	• Report of Colville/Tavistock study published • "Prospectus" in national press for loan stock.	
1974	• First Housing Action Area (HAA) in country declared for the Colville/Tavistock area • First purchases of property portfolios • Trust revenue deficit eligible for Revenue Deficit Grant from DoE • John Coward awarded OBE	• General Election, Labour Government elected • Housing Act enacted and led to huge growth in HA development and introduces new grants for both HA's policies and Housing Action Areas
1975	• 1000th house purchased • First HAA in Hammersmith and Fulham in Coningham Road area	
1976	• Two area committees established with tenant representation. • Large programme of HAAs initiated in Hammersmith and Fulham, with the Trust the lead association in 10 of them • 32 large properties bought for £1 million in Earls Court • Duchess of Gloucester becomes patron • Special projects unit established	• IMF asked for help by Government in financial crisis: public spending cuts followed
1977	• New Head Office opened at Paddenswick Road in Hammersmith • HRH Duke of Edinburgh visits Colville area	
1978	• 2000th home in Western Area	

1979	• First shared ownership in country at 88 Ladbroke Grove, opened by new Housing Minister, John Stanley
	• 2000th home in Kensington
	• First sheltered scheme completed
1980	• Trust in forefront of protest at Government moratorium on housing improvement
	• Addison Housing Association set up for shared ownership
	• NHHT Commercial Properties Limited established
	• NHHT Shops Limited established as separate company
1981	• 5000th home completed
1986	• John Coward retires
	• Archbishop of Canterbury opens St George's Community Trust hostel
	• Donald Hoodless appointed as new Chief Executive
	• All Saints Road almost a 'no go' area. Trust aimed to buy all houses in road to combat drugs and control use
1987	• Temporary Housing Team set up
	• Conversion of Apollo pub in All Saints Road into 16 small workshops is completed
1988	• Sir Roger Ormrod retires and Anthony Taussig succeeds as Chair.
	• Trust's silver jubilee celebrations, with 7876 homes in management
	• Addison completes its 1000th home
1989	• First sheltered scheme for ethnic minorities (Afro-Caribbean and Asian elders) opened

Right-hand column events:

• General Election and Conservative Government elected

• Housing Act 1980 introduced with Right to Buy

• Homelessness in London reached crisis proportions

• Housing Act 1988 passed, introduced private finance and low grants for housing associations. All new lettings on assured tenancies

1990	• Drayton Bridge Road handed over, the largest development to date at 252 homes • Private Finance Initiative scheme started as special project with Riverpoint • Rent Deposit Fund established • Business Expansion Scheme with RBKC • Mortgage Rescue in Mole Valley	• Homelessness increasing and Rough Sleeping initiative launched • Community Care Legislation
1992	• Responding to community care needs • New lettings procedures adopted • First Tenant Participation Officer • Colville Project established for ambitious regeneration scheme • 13 permanent shops	• Grant rates reducing impacting upon rent affordability • Government re-launches DIYSO
1993	• 30th anniversary • Consortium of associations plans 300 home development on sites of old Rootes factory • Commenced tackling stock reinvestment • Fundraising appeal launched in Kensington Palace • Donald Hoodless leaves	• Stock transfers commence in local authority sector • Government encourages tenant management and participation
1994	• Anthony Taussig retires as Chair and Lionel Morrison takes over • Peter Redman appointed as CEO • Rootes development started • Fundraising exceeds £500,000 • Scheme to build 30 homes funded by donations scheme	• NHF Inquiry into Governance and Nolan Committee on Standards in Public Life established
1995	• Home ownership had largest allocation from Housing Corporation • Fundraising exceeds £750,000 • John Kennedy Lodge opened in Islington	

- First Annual Report
to Tenants

1996
- Regeneration on Clem
Attlee estate started
- First Tenants Conference held
- Will Hutton debate

- 1996 Housing Act
enacted revising
Housing Associations
funding and procedures
and introducing
Right to Acquire
- Risk Management
becomes important

1997
- Lessees Forum set up by shared
ownership residents
- Fundraising opera
- Involvement commences in the
Carnival

- Labour Government
elected
- Social Exclusion
Unit set up

1998
- Group received largest capital
allocation by Housing Corporation
- New mixed tenure development at
Adastral Village completed
- Major fund raising for
St Christopher's hostel,
health centre and
jobs training.

- Crime and Disorder Act
enacted and protocols
with police established
- Human Rights Act
became law

1999
- Lionel Morrison stands down as
Chair and is succeeded by Lord
Sawyer of Darlington
- Chartermark for NHHO
- NGO Finance award for charitable
fundraising
- Lionel Morrison awarded OBE
- Investors in People awarded
- Committees restructured
- Dalgarno Project

2001
- Grahame Park development in
Barnet launched with local Council
- 360% Appraisals of Board members

- Housing Green Paper
published
- Neighbourhoods Unit
established

2002
- Passionate About Customer
Services Review completed
- Creation of Customer Panel

	• Neighbourhoods Boards replace Area Committees	• 2002 Homelessness Act became law
2003	• Audit Commission reports on inspection of Trust	
	• Peter Redman resigns as Chief Executive	
	• 50,000 people living in homes provided by Notting Hill Housing Group	
2004	• Kate Davies appointed as new Chief Executive	
	• Gerard Lemos appointed as Chair	

INDEX